P9-DHJ-589

Welcome to the
Reading/Writing
Workshop

Explore new ideas!

Read and reread exciting literature and informational texts!

Become an expert writer!

Use what you have learned to unlock the Wonders of reading!

Go Digital! www.connected.mcgraw-hill.com
Explore your Interactive Reading/Writing Workshop.

McGraw-Hill Reading

Wonders

McGraw Hill Education

Bothell, WA • Chicago, IL • Columbus, OH • New York, NY

Cover and Title Pages: Nathan Love

www.mheonline.com/readingwonders

B

The McGraw·Hill Companies

Education

Send all inquiries to:
McGraw-Hill Education
Two Penn Plaza
New York, New York 10121

ISBN: 978-0-02-118866-6
MHID: 0-02-118866-1

Printed in the United States of America.

7 8 9 DOW 17 16 15 14

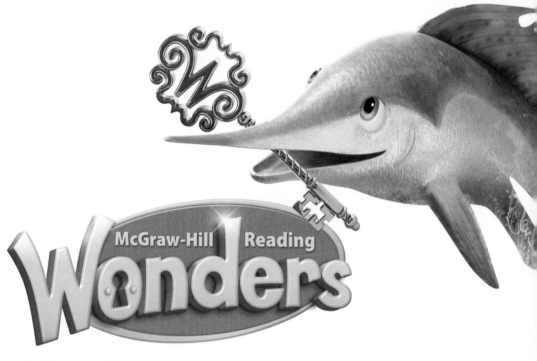

Wonders

McGraw-Hill Reading

CCSS Reading/Language Arts Program

Program Authors

Diane August

Donald R. Bear

Janice A. Dole

Jana Echevarria

Douglas Fisher

David Francis

Vicki Gibson

Jan Hasbrouck

Margaret Kilgo

Jay McTighe

Scott G. Paris

Timothy Shanahan

Josefina V. Tinajero

McGraw Hill Education

Bothell, WA • Chicago, IL • Columbus, OH • New York, NY

Unit 1 Friends and Family

The Big Idea

How do families and friends learn, grow, and help one another? **16**

(t) Tim Beaumont; (b) Janet Broxon

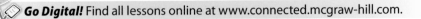 *Go Digital!* Find all lessons online at www.connected.mcgraw-hill.com.

(t) Marcin Piwowarski; (b) hana/Datacraft/imagenavi/Getty Images

SCIENCE

SOCIAL STUDIES

Unit 2 Animal Discoveries

The Big Idea

Go Digital! Find all lessons online at www.connected.mcgraw-hill.com.

Unit 3

Live and Learn

The Big Idea

What have you learned about the world that surprises you? **176**

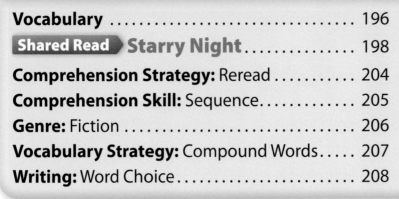

Go Digital! Find all lessons online at www.connected.mcgraw-hill.com.

Unit 4

Our Life Our World

The Big Idea

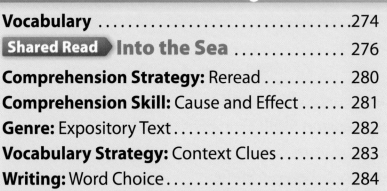

Go Digital! Find all lessons online at www.connected.mcgraw-hill.com.

(t) Corinna Ice; (c) Steven J. Kazlowski/Alamy; (b) Paul Thompson Images/Alamy

(t) Susan Swan; (c) Mike Litwin; : (b) nycShooter/Vetta/Getty Images

Unit 5

Let's Make a Difference

The Big Idea

How can people make a difference? **328**

Daniel Griffo

Go Digital! Find all lessons online at www.connected.mcgraw-hill.com.

(t) Margaret Lindmark; (c) Kristen Sorra; (b) Tetra Images/Getty Images

Unit 6

How on Earth?

The Big Idea
What keeps our world working? **400**

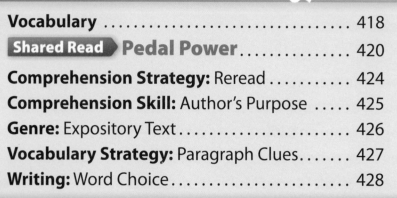

(t) Xiao Xin; (b) Jeremy Woodhouse/Blend Images/Corbis

Go Digital! Find all lessons online at www.connected.mcgraw-hill.com.

(t) Jeff Rotman/Photodisc/Getty Images; (b) Cat Zaza

15

Friends and Family

The Big Idea

How do families and friends learn, grow, and help one another?

Sonya Farrell/The Image Bank/Getty Images

Together Is Better

Baseball is no fun at all
    Without a friend to toss the ball.

Camping out would be a bore
    Without your brother to hear you snore.

Piano notes would sound all wrong.
    Without a friend to sing along.

Ice cream would not taste as sweet
    Without your sister to share the treat.

Cleaning up is hard to do
    Without your dad to help out too.

From morning until the day is done
    Friends and family make things fun.

by Constance Keremes

Essential Question

How do friends depend on each other?

Go Digital!

Friends
Help Each Other

These friends are helping each other find out where they are on the map. Their actions help each other. There are many ways we depend on our friends.

▶ We depend on our friends to teach us things.

▶ We need our friends to give us comfort when we are hurt or upset.

Talk About It

Talk with a partner about how friends depend on each other. Then write your ideas on the web.

Friends Depend on Each Other

Vocabulary

Use the picture and sentence to learn each word.

actions

The girl's **actions** helped her team win the soccer game.

What actions might help you do well in school?

afraid

Our dog is **afraid** of thunder.

What things are you afraid of?

depend

Nick **depends** on his dad to help him learn to ride a bike.

What do you depend on your parents for?

nervously

Maya waited **nervously** for her swim race to begin.

How would you look if you were acting nervously?

peered

The cat **peered** through the hole in the barn.

What would you see if you peered through a window at home?

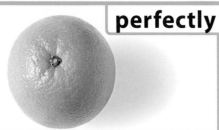

perfectly

The orange is **perfectly** round.

Name something in your house that is perfectly square.

rescue

We watched the boy **rescue** the cat from the tree.

What is another word for rescue?

secret

Mandy whispered a **secret** to me.

What is special about a secret?

COLLABORATE

Your Turn

Pick three words. Write three questions for your partner to answer.

Go Digital! *Use the online visual glossary*

Little Flap Learns to Fly

? Essential Question

How do friends depend on each other?

Read how Little Flap depends on his friends.

Little Flap was happy living in his nest. His friends, Fluff and Tuff, lived in the nest next to him. Every morning they sang songs together. Their parents brought them worms to eat.

One day Fluff asked, "Can we get our own worms?"

Tuff said, "We can if we learn to fly."

Fluff said, "Yes! Let's learn to fly."

Little Flap **peered** over the edge of his nest. It was very high up. When he looked down, the ground seemed very far away. He felt scared! He was too **afraid** to tell his friends about his fear so he kept his feelings a **secret**.

Fluff said, "Let's practice flapping our wings. It will make them strong. Watch."

Tuff and Little Flap watched Fluff. Then they copied her **actions**.

Soon it was time to fly. Little Flap could no longer keep his feelings a secret. He asked, "Will I fall? I don't want to get hurt."

Tuff said, "You can **depend** on Fluff and me. We're your friends."

Fluff said, "I have an idea. We will go first and show you how. Then you can try. If you fall, Tuff and I will **rescue** you."

Tuff said, "Yes, we can save you!" Tuff and Fluff jumped out of the nest. They flew!

Little Flap looked down **nervously**. He still felt uneasy, but he felt braver with his friends. "Okay," he said. "Let's try!"

The three birds stood together on the branch. They counted, "One! Two! Three!" Then they flapped their wings fast and jumped. Little Flap lifted into the air.

"You're flying just right!" said Fluff.

"You're flying **perfectly**!" said Tuff.

Tim Beaumont

All three little birds landed in a patch of soft, green grass.

Little Flap said, "Now I know I can always depend on you, Fluff and Tuff! You are my friends."

Then he found a big, juicy worm and shared it with his friends.

Now Little Flap likes flying!

Make Connections

Describe how Little Flap depends on his friends. ESSENTIAL QUESTION

Discuss a time when you depended on your friends. TEXT TO SELF

Visualize

When you visualize, you form pictures in your mind about the characters, setting, and events in the story.

Find Text Evidence

After reading page 23 of "Little Flap Learns to Fly," I know that Little Flap is thinking about flying. On page 24 what words does the author use to help readers visualize the nest?

page 24

Little Flap **peered** over the edge of his nest. It was very high up. When he looked down, the ground seemed very far

I read that the nest was very high up and the ground seemed far away. From this, I can visualize the nest.

Your Turn

COLLABORATE

Reread page 27. What words help you visualize where the birds landed?

Key Details

You can learn important information in a story by looking for key details in the illustrations.

 Find Text Evidence

As I read page 24 of "Little Flap Learns to Fly," I can look at the illustrations to find key details about the characters and events.

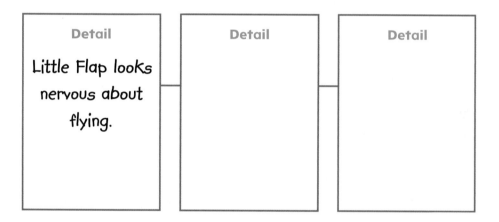

Detail	Detail	Detail
Little Flap looks nervous about flying.		

 COLLABORATE

Your Turn

Continue reading the story. Does Little Flap learn to fly? List the key details in your graphic organizer.

Go Digital!
Use the interactive graphic organizer

Fantasy

"Little Flap Learns to Fly" is a fantasy story.
A **Fantasy**:
- is a made-up story.
- has imaginary characters that could not be real.

Find Text Evidence

I can use what I read to tell that "Little Flap Learns to Fly" is a fantasy story. The story has made-up characters.

page 22

CCSS Shared Read   Genre • Fantasy

Little Flap
Learns
to Fly

Essential Question
How do friends depend on each other?
Read how Little Flap depends on his friends.

22

Use Illustrations

I see the birds have clothing on. I know birds in real life do not wear clothing. This must be fantasy.

COLLABORATE

Your Turn

Find two other things in the story that could not happen in real life. Tell why this story is a fantasy.

Inflectional Endings

To understand the meaning of a word you do not know, you can separate the root word from the ending, such as *-ed* or *-s*.

 Find Text Evidence

I'm not sure what the word looked *means. I know the root word* look *means "to see." The ending -ed means this action happened in the past. The word* looked *means "saw something in the past."*

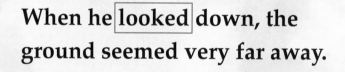

When he looked down, the ground seemed very far away.

Your Turn

Use the endings to figure out the meanings of these words in "Little Flap Learns to Fly."
friends, *page 24*
counted, *page 26*

Tim Beaumont

31

Readers to . . .

Writers share their ideas by giving details about one thing or event at a time. Reread the passage from "Little Flap Learns to Fly."

Expert Model

Ideas

What **event** does the writer tell about? How do the details make her **ideas** clear?

Little Flap peered over the edge of his nest. It was very high up. When he looked down, the ground seemed very far away. He felt scared! He was too afraid to tell his friends about his fear so he kept his feelings a secret.

Writers

Kelly wrote a story about animal friends. Read Kelly's revisions.

Editing Marks

≡ Make a capital letter.

ℐ Take out.

∧ Add.

Grammar Handbook
Sentences
See page 474.

Student Model

Help from a Friend

Lori Lamb went to the park with s̲am Sheep. Lori was on the swing. Sam pushed Lori too high. She sailed into the top of a tall tree. Who would save her^? Sam was too small. Their friend Greg Giraffe was eating leaves at a nearby tree. Sam called for help. Greg ~~got~~ ∧saved Lori!

Your Turn

COLLABORATE

☑ Identify the event Kelly describes.
☑ Identify one statement and one question.
☑ Tell how revisions improved her writing.

Go Digital!
Write online in Writer's Workspace

? **Essential Question**

How are families around the world the same and different?

Go Digital!

Families Celebrate

In some parts of the world, families celebrate a holiday called Holi. During Holi, families celebrate Spring.

▶ Families use colored powder on each other to celebrate flowers blooming.

▶ Families share a big meal.

Talk About It

Talk with a partner about how your family celebrations are the same and different. Write your ideas on the chart.

Same	Different

Vocabulary

Use the picture and sentence to learn each word.

aside

Juan moves **aside** books on the shelf to find one he likes.

Describe why a person might move aside.

culture

At Chinese New Year, we learn about our **culture**.

Tell about a holiday that shows your culture.

fair

Mom cut the cake so we all got our **fair** share.

What does it mean to be fair?

invited

I **invited** some friends to my birthday party.

Tell about an event you were invited to.

language My friend Naomi speaks and writes in another **language**.

What languages do you know?

plead I had to **plead** with Dad to get a new bike.

What is something you might plead for?

scurries The squirrel **scurries** across the yard.

What is the opposite of scurries?

share I like to **share** music with my sister.

Describe something you share with a family member.

COLLABORATE

Your Turn

Pick three words. Write three questions for your partner to answer.

Go Digital! **Use the online visual glossary**

(t) Christopher Pillitz/Corbis; (tc) Stewart Cohen/Pam Ostrow/Getty Images; (bc) PetStockBoys/Alamy; (b) Mark Edward Atkinson/Getty Images

Maria Celebrates Brazil

? Essential Question

How are families around the world the same and different?

Read about a family from Brazil.

Maria and her family are in their bright, hot kitchen. "Please, Mãe, por favor!" Maria begs.

Mãe speaks Portuguese. This is the **language** of Brazil. "No matter how much you beg or **plead**, you must go to practice. The parade is next week."

"It's not **fair**," says Maria in English.

Mãe does not know a lot of English. Maria is surprised when she asks, "What is not fair about going to practice? You must do the right thing."

"Ana **invited** me to her house," Maria answers. "I want to go!"

Pai says, "Maria, the parade is important. People from around the world come to see it. They try our food, see how we dress, and how we live. It is a chance for us to **share** our **culture**."

"I know but I really want to see Ana," says Maria.

Pai says, "Maria, you can see Ana another time. They are giving out costumes at practice today."

Maria thinks about her father's words. Pai is right. She and the other children have worked hard for a year. They practiced their dance steps over and over. They even made their own bright colorful costumes.

"You're right," Maria says to her father. "I'll go to practice. I'll tell Ana I cannot visit her."

One week passes. Lots of people line the streets. The children in Maria's group are wearing their sparkling costumes. They know each dance step. They dance to the beat.

Janet Broxon

The crowd moves **aside** as they make their way down the street.

When the crowd moves away, Maria sees a woman with a camera. She is hurrying. The woman **scurries** by Maria. She puts her camera to her eye. Maria smiles from ear to ear. She is excited to be in the parade. Click! The woman takes a picture of Maria. Maria is proud of her hard work!

Make Connections

How is Maria's family the same and different from other families you know? ESSENTIAL QUESTION

Compare Maria's family to your own family. TEXT TO SELF

Visualize

When you visualize, you use the author's words to form pictures in your mind about a story.

Find Text Evidence

On page 41 of "Maria Celebrates Brazil," what words does the author use to help you visualize the costumes?

page 41

Maria thinks about her father's words. Pai is right. She and the other children have worked hard for a year. They practiced their dance steps over and over. They even made their own bright colorful costumes.

I read that the children made bright and colorful costumes. This helps me visualize the parade.

Your Turn

COLLABORATE

What does Maria do in the parade? Reread page 42 and visualize parts of the story that help you answer the question.

Janet Broxon

Character, Setting, Events

A character is a person or animal in a story. The setting of a story tells when and where a story takes place. The events are what happens.

Find Text Evidence

*As I read page 39 of "Maria Celebrates Brazil,"
I learn who the characters are, what they do,
and where the story takes place.*

Character	Setting	Events
Maria, Mãe Pai	Maria's Kitchen	Maria wants to miss practice to go to her friend's house.

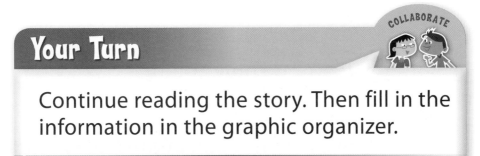

Your Turn

Continue reading the story. Then fill in the information in the graphic organizer.

Go Digital!
Use the interactive graphic organizer

Realistic Fiction

The story "*Maria Celebrates Brazil*," is realistic fiction. **Realistic fiction**:

- is a made-up story with characters that could be real people.
- has a beginning, middle, and end.

Find Text Evidence

I can tell that "Maria Celebrates Brazil" is realistic fiction. The characters are like real people. Also, the story has a beginning, middle and end.

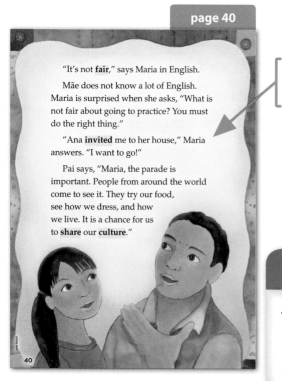

page 40

"It's not **fair**," says Maria in English.

Mãe does not know a lot of English. Maria is surprised when she asks, "What is not fair about going to practice? You must do the right thing."

"Ana **invited** me to her house," Maria answers. "I want to go!"

Pai says, "Maria, the parade is important. People from around the world come to see it. They try our food, see how we dress, and how we live. It is a chance for us to **share** our **culture**."

40

Story Structure

In the beginning of the story, I read that Maria wants to skip practice and go to a friend's house.

Your Turn

COLLABORATE

Tell about events that happen in the middle and end of the story.

Root Words

To understand the meaning of a word you do not know, try to separate the root word from the endings such as *–ed*, or *-ing*.

 Find Text Evidence

As I read the word hurrying, *I can split the root word* hurry *from the ending* -ing, *which can mean something happening right now. I think* hurrying *means "moving quickly right now."*

> **Maria sees a woman with a camera. She is** hurrying.

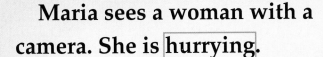

Your Turn COLLABORATE

Use root words to figure out the meanings of other words in *"Maria Celebrates Brazil."*
  worked, *page 41*
  practiced, *page 41*

Janet Broxon

Readers to...

Good writers make sure they create a strong beginning by telling about the characters and the problem they are facing. Reread the passage from "Maria Celebrates Brazil."

Strong Beginning Identify important details about the characters and events. How do these details create a **strong beginning**?

Expert Model

Maria and her family are in their bright, hot kitchen. "Please, Mãe, por favor!" Maria begs.

Mãe speaks Portuguese. This is the language of Brazil. "No matter how much you beg or plead, you must go to practice. The parade is next week."

Writers

Petra wrote a realistic fiction story. Read Petra's revisions.

Editing Marks

∧ Add

⊙ Add a period.

⌒ Take out.

≡ Make a capital letter.

Grammar Handbook

Commands and Exclamations
See page 474.

Student Model

♫ ♪ Jan's Show

It was the night of Jan's ∧big dance show. Her legs didn't feel steady⊙ jan had been practicing all month.

"I know I can do this∧!" Jan thought. She heard the music start. Jan took a deep breath and smiled. Her legs ~~felt fine~~∧weren't shaking any more.

Your Turn

☑ Identify the sentences that show a strong beginning.
☑ Identify an exclamation.
☑ Tell how revisions improved her writing.

Go Digital!
Write online in Writer's Workspace

Essential Question

How can a pet be an important friend?

Go Digital!

Our Pet Friends

Pets can be our friends. Pets come in all shapes and sizes.

▶ Pets can make us laugh.

▶ Pets can help us.

▶ Pets love us.

Talk About It

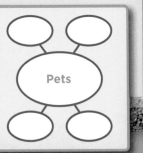

Talk with a partner about having pets as friends. Write words on the word web that tell how pets are our friends.

Pets

Vocabulary

Use the picture and sentence to learn each word.

decide

I **decide** to have juice and cereal for breakfast.

What did you decide to eat for breakfast today?

different

The brown kitten is **different** than the orange kitten.

How are a horse and a cat different?

friendship

Because of their **friendship**, the kids played together a lot.

Tell about your friendship with a friend.

glance

I **glance** to see what book my sister is reading.

What word is the opposite of glance?

proper　It is **proper** to wipe your mouth during a meal.

Tell how to act in a proper way at the library.

relationship　Our teacher has a good **relationship** with our class.

What relationship do you have with your best friend?

stares　Helen **stares** at her friend.

What do you look like when you stare at something?

trade　Don and Luis **trade** baseball cards.

What things do you trade with your friend?

COLLABORATE

Your Turn

Pick three words. Write three questions for your partner to answer.

Go Digital! **Use the online visual glossary**

Finding Cal

Essential Question

How can a pet be an important friend?

Read about a dog who becomes a boy's special friend.

Dear Diary,

It took Dad a long time to **decide**. He finally made up his mind. Dad came to my room tonight. He said I could get a dog! But it has to be a small or medium-sized dog. We will go to the animal shelter tomorrow.

Medium Dog

Small Dog

Dear Diary,

September 26

Wow! There are so many **different** dogs at the shelter. There are big and little dogs. Some have soft fur and some have wiry hair.

Dad and I walked to one dog's cage. The tag said the dog's name was Cal. One quick **glance** at the cute dog, and I knew he was for me. Dad said, "Look, Jake! Look at how Cal **stares** at you." It was true! His eyes were wide open. He was looking right at me.

Jack Spot Sam Cal

Marcin Piwowarski

We put Cal on a leash and took him to a fenced yard. Cal smiled and stared at me. Cal wanted to play. In minutes he learned the **proper**, or correct, way to sit. He could walk on a leash nicely, too. I patted him on the head, and he licked my hand.

Cal licking my hand!

Dad said, "I see a real connection between you and Cal." I agreed. We already had a good **relationship**.

Soon we were on our way home. Cal was nervous so I tried to make him feel better. I scratched his ears, and he liked it.

October 10

Dear Diary,

It has been a while since I have written. Cal has learned many new tricks like how to roll over. I have learned from Cal, too.

Cal's Tricks!

Cal walks with Dad and me to school every day. Each night, Dad reads me a story. Cal lies next to me. I would not **trade** him for any other dog. I will keep him because our **friendship** is very special. Finding Cal was worth the wait!

 ## Make Connections

How is Cal an important friend to Jake? ESSENTIAL QUESTION

Compare Jake's pet Cal to your pet or a pet you know. Tell how each pet is a good friend. TEXT TO SELF

Ask and Answer Questions

When you read, you can ask questions to help you think about parts of the story that you may have missed or do not understand.

🔍 Find Text Evidence

After reading page 56 of "Finding Cal," I ask myself, "What helped Jake decide to take Cal home?"

page 57

to a fenced yard. Cal smiled and stared at me. Cal wanted to play. In minutes he learned the **proper**, or correct, way to sit. He could walk on a leash nicely, too. I patted him on the head, and he licked my hand.

Cal licking my hand!

I read that Cal smiled and stared at Jake. Cal wants to play with Jake. From this, I understand that Cal is already special to Jake.

Your Turn
COLLABORATE

Think of a question you have about the story. Reread the parts of the story that help you answer the question.

Character, Setting, Events

The pictures and text give you details about the characters, setting, and events in a story.

 Find Text Evidence

As I look at the pictures and read the text on page 55 of "Finding Cal," I see details about the character, setting, and events.

Character	Setting	Events
Jake	Jake's Home	Jake is excited to be getting a dog.

Your Turn

Continue reading the story. Then fill in the information in the graphic organizer.

Go Digital!
Use the interactive graphic organizer

Fiction

The story "Finding Cal" is Fiction. Fiction:
- has made up characters and events.
- has a beginning, middle, and end.

Find Text Evidence

I can use what I read to tell that "Finding Cal" is fiction. The story has a beginning, middle, and end.

page 55

Dear Diary,

September 25

It took Dad a long time to **decide**. He finally made up his mind. Dad came to my room tonight. He said I could get a dog! But it has to be a small or medium-sized dog. We will go to the animal shelter tomorrow.

Medium Dog

Small Dog

55

Story Structure

In the beginning of the story, I read that a family decides to adopt a dog.

COLLABORATE

Your Turn

Tell about events that happen in the middle and end of the story.

Context Clues

To understand the meaning of a word you do not know, look at the other words in the sentence for clues.

 Find Text Evidence

I'm not sure what the word "nervous" means. The words "make him feel better" make me think Cal was not relaxed. I think "nervous" means not relaxed.

Cal was nervous so I tried to make him feel better.

COLLABORATE

Your Turn

Use context clues to figure out the meanings of other words in "Finding Cal."
connection, *page 58*
leash, *page 57*

Marcin Piwowarski

63

Readers to...

Writers choose precise words to help paint clear pictures in the reader's mind. Reread the passage from "Finding Cal".

Expert Model

Word Choice
Identify two **precise** words. Why are these words good examples of **word choice**?

Wow! There are so many different dogs at the shelter. There are big and little dogs. Some have soft fur and some have wiry hair.

Dad and I walked to one dog's cage.

Marcin Piwowarski

Writers

Grammar Handbook

Subjects see page 475.

Jared wrote a letter to his friend. Read Jared's letter.

Student Model

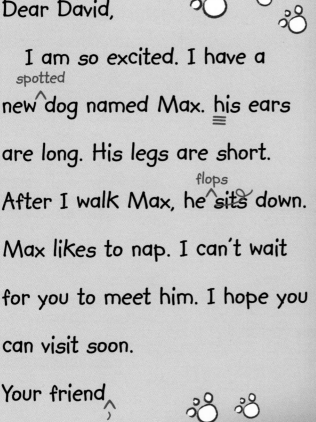

Dear David,

I am so excited. I have a
spotted
new ∧ dog named Max. his ears
           ≡≡≡

are long. His legs are short.

                    flops
After I walk Max, he ∧ sits down.

Max likes to nap. I can't wait

for you to meet him. I hope you

can visit soon.

Your friend ∧

Jared

Your Turn   COLLABORATE

- ☑ Identify the precise words Jared used.
- ☑ Identify the subjects.
- ☑ Tell how the revisions improved his writing.

Go Digital!
Write online in Writer's Workspace

65

Essential Question

How do we care for animals?

Go Digital!

Caring for Animals

All animals have needs. People give the animals what they need to live.

Animals need:

▶ fresh food and water each day

▶ air to breathe

▶ a safe place to live

Talk About It

Work with a partner. Tell how people care for animals. Write your ideas on the word web.

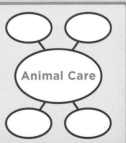

Animal Care

Vocabulary

Use the picture and sentence to learn each word.

allowed

Dogs are not **allowed** on the beach.

What things are allowed at school?

care

I help **care** for my little brother.

Tell how you take care of your belongings.

excited

The girls were **excited** to play with their new puppy.

What would you be excited about seeing or doing?

needs

Food and water are some of the **needs** of every animal.

What are your needs?

roam Lions **roam** the plains in Africa.

Describe how you move when you roam.

safe Wearing a seatbelt keeps me **safe** in the car.

How can you stay safe when riding a bike?

wandered A bear cub **wandered** away from its mother.

What is the opposite of wandered?

wild Bears and raccoons live in the **wild**.

Name some animals you have seen in the wild.

COLLABORATE

Your Turn

Pick three words. Write three questions for your partner to answer.

Go Digital! **Use the online visual glossary**

Taking Care of
Pepper

Alaska Stock Images/National Geographic Stock

Essential Question

How do we care for animals?

Read about how a boy cares for a horse.

Have you ever been on a farm? Jack lives on a farm. He has a horse named Pepper. Jack helps take **care** of Pepper. Looking after a horse is a big job. A horse has many **needs**. There are a lot of things a horse must have to live.

Pepper stomps his hoof and nods his head when he sees Jack.

Every morning, Jack wakes up at 5:00 a.m. He and his father go to Pepper's stall. The stall keeps Pepper **safe** from bad weather and other dangers.

When Pepper sees Jack, the horse gets **excited**. Jack smiles when the horse gets all worked up.

First, Jack gives Pepper hay to eat. While Pepper eats, Jack cleans Pepper's stall. He shovels out the dirty hay and sawdust. Then he puts down fresh padding.

Next, Jack strokes Pepper's brown coat and it feels smooth. Then Jack leaves to go to school. But his work is not done!

At 3:00 p.m., Jack rides the bus back home. He has a snack and does his homework. Next, his mother gives him an apple for Pepper. Then they go to visit Pepper.

Jack feeds Pepper hay and fresh water every day.

Jack and his mom find Pepper in a field. Pepper is **allowed** to **roam**. He can walk all around the field. He was drinking after having **wandered** the field. All that walking here and there made Pepper thirsty!

Now it is time for Pepper's exercise. In the **wild**, horses run many hours a day. But Pepper does not live out in nature. Jack must make sure Pepper gets the exercise he needs.

Pepper must have exercise each day.

Carol Walker/naturepl.com

Jack puts the saddle on Pepper. He places the bit in Pepper's mouth. Mom does the same thing with her horse, and they ride horses together.

Jack's Dad checks for rocks in Pepper's hooves. If he sees one, he must get it out.

When they are finished riding, Jack grooms Pepper. He brushes his mane, tail, and fur.

Finally, Jack gives Pepper more hay and refills his water bucket. "See you in the morning," Jack says. Pepper nods his head as if to say, "Yes, I'll be waiting!"

Make Connections

How do people care for horses? **ESSENTIAL QUESTION**

Compare the needs of a horse and another pet you know. Which needs more care? **TEXT TO SELF**

Ask and Answer Questions

When you read, asking questions helps you think about parts of the story you may have missed or do not understand.

 Find Text Evidence

On page 71 of "Taking Care of Pepper," I read that a horse has many needs. I ask myself, "What things does a horse need?"

page 72

> Every morning, Jack wakes up at 5:00 a.m. He and his father go to Pepper's stall. The stall keeps Pepper **safe** from bad weather and other dangers.
>
> When Pepper sees Jack, the horse gets **excited**. Jack smiles when the horse gets all worked up.
>
> First, Jack gives Pepper hay to eat. While Pepper eats, Jack cleans Pepper's stall. He shovels out the dirty hay and sawdust. Then he puts down fresh padding.
>
> 72

I read that Jack feeds Pepper hay. I understand that Jack takes care of Pepper and gives him what he needs.

Your Turn

COLLABORATE

Think of a question to ask about Pepper's needs. Reread parts of the selection to find the answer to the question.

Key Details

You can find important details in the photos and text of a selection.

 Find Text Evidence

As I read the text and photo caption on page 72 of "Taking Care of Pepper," I understand that Jack cares for Pepper. Pepper recognizes Jack and shows that he cares for him, too.

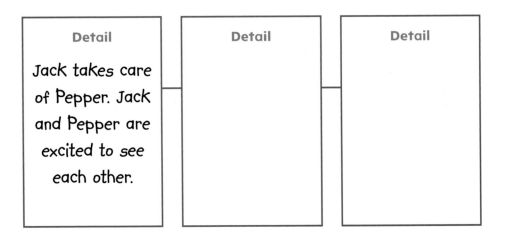

Detail	Detail	Detail
Jack takes care of Pepper. Jack and Pepper are excited to see each other.		

COLLABORATE

Your Turn

Continue reading the selection. Then fill in the information in the graphic organizer.

Go Digital!
Use the interactive graphic organizer

Narrative Nonfiction

The selection "Taking Care of Pepper" is a Narrative Nonfiction. A **Narrative Nonfiction**:

- is about real people, things, or events.
- is told by a narrator.
- can have photos and captions.

Find Text Evidence

I know that "Taking Care of Pepper" is a narrative nonfiction because it tells how a boy cares for a real horse. The photos and captions tell more about how to care for a horse.

page 72

Pepper stomps his hoof and nods his head when he sees Jack.

Every morning, Jack wakes up at 5:00 a.m. He and his father go to Pepper's stall. The stall keeps Pepper **safe** from bad weather and other dangers.

When Pepper sees Jack, the horse gets **excited**. Jack smiles when the horse gets all worked up.

First, Jack gives Pepper hay to eat. While Pepper eats, Jack cleans Pepper's stall. He shovels out the dirty hay and sawdust. Then he puts down fresh padding.

72

Text Features

- **Photos** are pictures.
- **Captions** are words that tell about a photo.

Your Turn COLLABORATE

Find other photos with captions. Tell what you learn from them.

Root Words

To understand the meaning of a word you do not know, try to break up the word into word parts. You can split the root word from the ending such as *–ed*, *-es*, or *-ing*.

 Find Text Evidence

As I read the word finished, *I can break out the root word* finish, *which means "to come to an end," from the ending -ed, which can mean "happened in the past." I think the word* finished *means "came to an end."*

> When they are finished riding, Jack grooms Pepper.

COLLABORATE

Your Turn

Use root words to figure out the meanings of other words in "Taking Care of Pepper."
brushes, *page 75*
waiting, *page 75*

Readers to . . .

Writers put their ideas in an order, or sequence, using words such as *first*, *next*, *then*, and *last*. Reread the passage from "Taking Care of Pepper."

Organization
Sequence
Identify the words that show the sequence. How do these words help you?

Expert Model

First, Jack gives Pepper hay to eat. While Pepper eats, Jack cleans Pepper's stall. He shovels out the dirty hay and sawdust. Then he puts down fresh padding.

Next, Jack strokes Pepper's brown coat and it feels smooth. Then Jack leaves to go to school. But his work is not done!

Writers

Mia wrote an informational text. Read Mia's revision.

Editing Marks

∧   Add

⊙   Add a period.

/   Make lowercase.

Grammar Handbook

Predicates

See page 475.

Student Model

Caring for a Dog

A dog needs love and care.

First, take your dog for a walk

each morning. ∧^Then Give him food

and water.

Take your dog for another

walk in the evening. Remember

to play with your dog ⊙ Give him

∧ ^Last,

a bath when he is dirty. ∧Take

him to the vet once a year.

Your Turn

COLLABORATE

☑ Identify the sequence words Mia used.

☑ Identify predicates.

☑ Tell how revisions improved her writing.

Go Digital!
Write online in Writer's Workspace

? Essential Question

What happens when families work together?

Go Digital!

How Families Work

This family is working together to make a pie. Working together gets chores done and can be fun! There are many ways families work together.

▶ Families do jobs at home, such as cooking and cleaning.

▶ Families shop together for food and clothing. They think about the cost of the items.

Talk About It

Talk with a partner about how your family works together. List your ideas on the web.

Families Work Together

Vocabulary

Use the picture and sentence to learn each word.

check Mom will **check** to make sure Tina's helmet fits.

When would you need to check something?

choose Julian will **choose** a shirt to wear.

Tell about a time when you had to choose something.

chores Sierra must finish her **chores** before she can play.

What is another word for chores?

cost Jordan asked, "How much does the shirt **cost**?"

What are two things that cost a lot of money?

customers

The **customers** lined up to buy lemonade.

Why would a store like to have a lot of customers?

jobs

Nurse and doctor are two **jobs** at a hospital.

Name some other jobs people have.

spend

William decided to **spend** his money on a snack.

Name two things parents spend their money on.

tools

Tom and his dad used **tools** to build a birdhouse.

What are some tools you have seen people use?

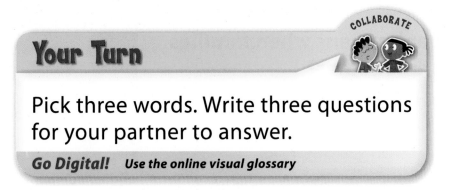

Your Turn

COLLABORATE

Pick three words. Write three questions for your partner to answer.

Go Digital! *Use the online visual glossary*

Masterfile

Essential Question

What happens when families work together?

Read about how one family works to meets their needs.

Families Work!

Ellen Yung had a busy day at work! She put a cast on a broken arm, used a bandage to cover a deep cut, and helped twenty patients. Ellen is a doctor for children. **Customers** can get sick at any time, so pediatricians work long hours. They have hard **jobs**.

Ellen's husband works long hours, too. Steve is a firefighter. At the fire house, he makes sure the **tools** work properly. He **checks** the hoses and fire trucks. At the fire, Steve rescues people from hot flames and smoke. The firefighters all work together to put out the fire.

When a fire alarm sounds, Steve suits up quickly.

At home, the Yung family works together too. Hanna sets the table for dinner. She also helps wash the dishes. Everyone has weekly **chores**. Mom and Hanna do the dusting and mopping. Dad and her brother, Zac, do the laundry. They wash, dry, and fold the clothes. Mom makes a shopping list each week. She lists items they need and things they want.

A short time ago, Zac wanted a new laptop. The family needed a new washing machine. They could only **spend** money on one item. Both **cost** the same. They had to **choose**. Clean clothes are needed for school and work. A new laptop is nice, but did Zac need it? Ellen and Steve thought about their family's needs. They decided to buy the washing machine.

Hanna's brother, Zac, helps with the meals.

What Are Some Needs and Wants?

Needs	Wants
Water	Skateboard
Food	Video game
Shelter	Basketball
Clothing	

Zac knows that his parents have busy jobs. They bring home money to pay for their needs and wants. They needed that washing machine. Zac still wants a laptop. The family has decided to save some money each week so they can buy it in the future.

Make Connections

How does the Yung family work together? **ESSENTIAL QUESTION**

How is your family similar or different from the family in the story? **TEXT TO SELF**

Ask and Answer Questions

When you read, asking questions helps you think about parts of the story you may have missed or do not understand.

Find Text Evidence

As I read page 88 of "Families Work!" I ask myself, "Why did the family buy a washing machine instead of a laptop?" I will reread to find the answer to my question.

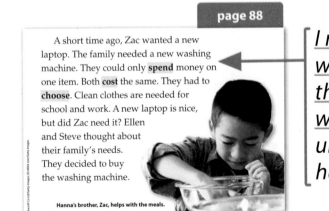

page 88

A short time ago, Zac wanted a new laptop. The family needed a new washing machine. They could only **spend** money on one item. Both **cost** the same. They had to **choose**. Clean clothes are needed for school and work. A new laptop is nice, but did Zac need it? Ellen and Steve thought about their family's needs. They decided to buy the washing machine.

Hanna's brother, Zac, helps with the meals.

I read that Zac wanted a laptop, but the family needed a washing machine. I understand the family had to make a choice.

COLLABORATE

Think of a question you have about the story. Reread the parts of the selection to find the answer to the question.

Key Details

Key details are important pieces of information in a text. Key details are found in the text and photos of a selection.

 Find Text Evidence

As I read and look at the photos on pages 86 and 87 of "Families Work!" I understand that Ellen Yung is a pediatrician. Her husband, Steve, is a firefighter. They both work away from home.

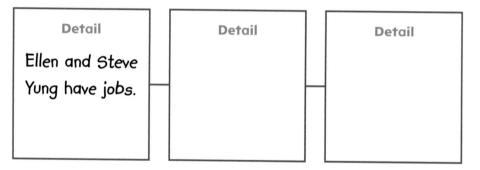

Detail	Detail	Detail
Ellen and Steve Yung have jobs.		

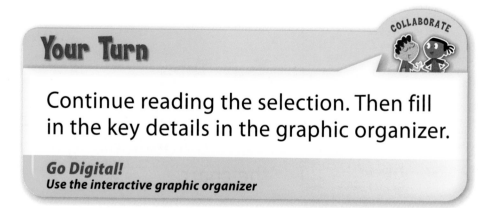

Your Turn

COLLABORATE

Continue reading the selection. Then fill in the key details in the graphic organizer.

Go Digital!
Use the interactive graphic organizer

Expository Text

"Families Work!" is an expository text.
Expository text:
- gives facts and information about a topic.
- can have text features.

🔍 Find Text Evidence

I know "Families Work!" is expository text because it gives facts about how family members work to meet their needs. It also has text features.

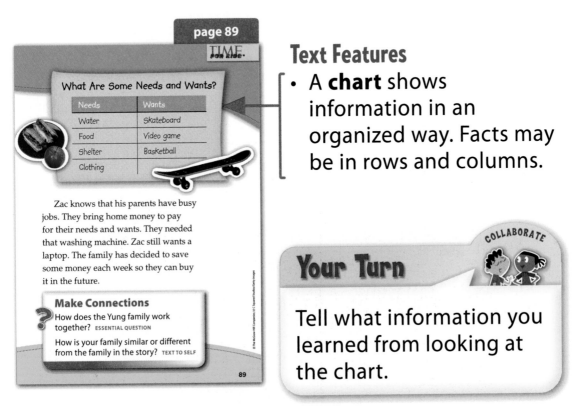

page 89

TIME FOR KIDS.

What Are Some Needs and Wants?

Needs	Wants
Water	Skateboard
Food	Video game
Shelter	Basketball
Clothing	

Zac knows that his parents have busy jobs. They bring home money to pay for their needs and wants. They needed that washing machine. Zac still wants a laptop. The family has decided to save some money each week so they can buy it in the future.

Make Connections

How does the Yung family work together? ESSENTIAL QUESTION

How is your family similar or different from the family in the story? TEXT TO SELF

89

Text Features

- A **chart** shows information in an organized way. Facts may be in rows and columns.

Your Turn COLLABORATE

Tell what information you learned from looking at the chart.

Inflectional Endings

To understand the meaning of a word you do not know, separate the root word from its ending, such as *-s, -es,* or *-ed.*

 Find Text Evidence

I see the word dishes. *I can separate the root word* dish, *which means "a plate or bowl used for holding food," from the inflectional ending* -es, *which can mean "more than one." I think the word* dishes *means "more than one dish."*

She also helps wash the dishes.

 COLLABORATE

Your Turn

Name the inflectional ending and the meaning of these words in "Families Work!":
  hours, *page 87*
  helped, *page 87*

Readers to...

Writers use long and short sentences in their writing. This makes their writing more interesting. Reread the passage from "Families Work!"

Expert Model

Sentence Fluency
Identify two **sentence types**. How do they help the writing?

Both cost the same. They had to choose. Clean clothes are needed for school and work. A new laptop is nice, but did Zac need it? Ellen and Steve thought about their family's needs. They decided to buy the washing machine.

Writers

Josh wrote an expository text. Read Josh's revision.

Editing Marks

∧ Add

⌟ Take out.

⊙ Add a period

Grammar Handbook

Combining Sentences
See page 476.

Student Model

Families Get It Done

Mr. Moore is a principal.
What happens when they go home?
Mrs. Moore is a chef.∧At

home, there is more work to

do⊙∧Their children help. Martha

and
helps cook,⌟Sam helps wash

dishes. The whole family

works together to get

everything done!

Your Turn

COLLABORATE

- ☑ Identify the sentence types Josh used.
- ☑ Find two sentences Josh combined.
- ☑ Tell how revisions improved his writing.

Go Digital!
Write online in Writer's Workspace

95

Animal Discoveries

The Big Idea

How do animals play a part in the world around us?

Animals Are Amazing

Kittens mew and dogs play catch,
Ducks and hens lay eggs to hatch.
    Animals are amazing!

Bees make honey, lambs give wool,
Horses gallop, oxen pull.

Big game lions prowl and roar,
Turtles crawl and eagles soar.

Animals at work and play,
All around me, night and day.
    Animals are amazing!

by Winifred Califano

? Essential Question

How do animals survive?

Go Digital!

Animal Survival

Meerkats live in hot, dry places. Here are some ways they adapt to the heat.

► They live in underground burrows.

► They have thin fur.

► They search for food in the early morning hours when it is cool.

Talk About It

Talk with a partner about how animals survive in hot climates. Write your ideas on the web.

Vocabulary

Use the picture and sentence to learn each word.

adapt
The polar bear's thick fur coat helps it **adapt** to the icy water.

How do you adapt to cold weather?

climate
Tom lives in a hot and sunny **climate**.

What is the climate like where you live?

eager
Mindy is **eager** to see her grandmother.

What is something that you are eager to do?

freedom
Deer have the **freedom** to move about the open land.

What animals are free to roam about the forest?

fresh

The baker made **fresh** bread every day.

What word means the opposite of *fresh*?

sense

I felt a **sense** of pride when I won the race.

When do you feel a *sense* of pride?

shadows

We made animal **shadows** on the wall.

What *shadows* can you make?

silence

The baby needed **silence** to fall asleep.

What word means the same as *silence*?

Your Turn

COLLABORATE

Pick three words. Write three questions for your partner to answer.

Go Digital! **Use the online visual glossary**

CCSS Shared Read Genre • Realistic Fiction

A Visit to the Desert

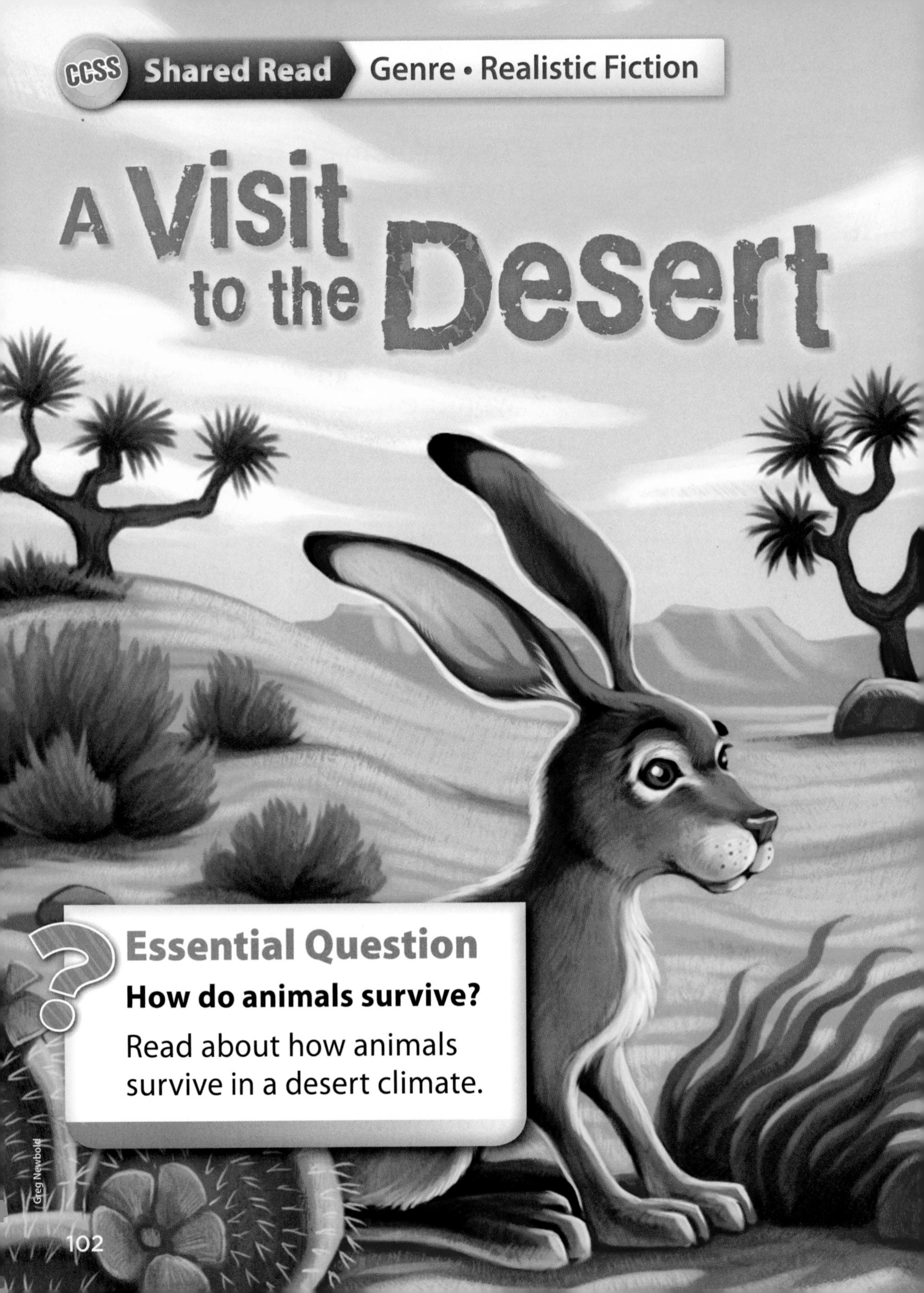

Essential Question

How do animals survive?

Read about how animals survive in a desert climate.

Greg Newbold

Tim was looking forward to this vacation. Then his parents told him the family would be visiting Grandma in Nevada. Tim was unhappy. He wanted to be with his friends this summer.

"Grandma is **eager** to see you," Mom said. "She can't wait to take you on a desert hike."

The next morning Grandma met them at the airport. Then they drove to the desert. As they hiked, Grandma explained that animals enjoy the open desert space. It gives them the **freedom** to move from place to place. Tim learned that the animals find ways to **adapt** to the hot desert weather. He wondered if he could get used to the desert **climate**.

Greg Newbold

"Wow," Tim said, "look at that! The turtle carries its home on its back!"

Grandma smiled at Tim's excitement. "Actually," she said, "that is a desert tortoise. It looks for the shade made by the **shadows** of rocks. That's how it cools off. He burrows underground to get away from the heat." The tortoise disappeared into its burrow. Tim leaned over the hole. He could not hear a sound.

"I'll bet it likes the **silence** of its burrow," Tim whispered.

"I think it likes its **sense** of safety too," Grandma added.

"That's the same feeling I get at home," Tim sighed. Just then a large rabbit hopped by. Grandma explained that the jack rabbit's large ears help it stay cool.

"These animals are so unlike the animals at home!" Tim said. He had forgotten about the desert heat.

"Some animals stay cool by sleeping during the day. Then they hunt at night," said Grandma. A Great Horned Owl hooted above them. Grandma said, "It will soon be time for the owl to hunt."

Greg Newbold

"Which means it's time for us to head back," Dad added.

"Aw, this vacation is going by too fast," Tim said. They asked Tim about the heat. "What heat?" Tim asked. "I feel as **fresh** and cool as a new flower. I've adapted!" Everyone laughed.

Make Connections

How does the desert tortoise survive in the heat? **ESSENTIAL QUESTION**

Think of another animal you know. How does it survive in its climate? **TEXT TO SELF**

Make Predictions

Use what you already know and what you read in the story to help you predict, or guess, what might happen next.

 Find Text Evidence

After reading page 104 of "A Visit to the Desert," I predicted that Tim would enjoy his visit to the desert. I kept reading to confirm my prediction.

---

page 105

"Wow," Tim said, "Look at that! The turtle carries its home on its back!"

Grandma smiled at Tim's excitement. "Actually," she said. "That is a desert tortoise. It looks for the shade made by the **shadows** of rocks. That's how it cools off. He burrows underground to get away from the heat." The tortoise disappeared into its burrow. Tim leaned over the hole. He could not hear a sound.

On page 105, I read that Tim was excited to learn about different desert animals. I confirmed my prediction.

Your Turn

Reread page 105. What did you predict would happen next? Look for clues in the text to decide if your prediction was correct.

Greg Newbold

Plot

The plot is the events that happen in the beginning, middle and end of the story.

 Find Text Evidence

When I read "A Visit to the Desert," I think about the plot, or what happens in the story.

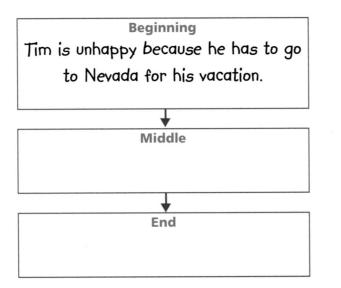

Beginning

Tim is unhappy because he has to go to Nevada for his vacation.

↓

Middle

↓

End

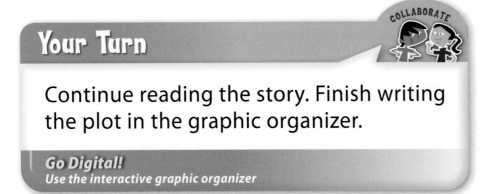

COLLABORATE

Your Turn

Continue reading the story. Finish writing the plot in the graphic organizer.

Go Digital!
Use the interactive graphic organizer

Realistic Fiction

The story "A Visit to the Desert" is realistic fiction. **Realistic fiction**:
- is a story that could happen in real life.
- has characters that could be real people.

Find Text Evidence

I can tell from the text that "A Visit to the Desert" is realistic fiction. Tim acts like a real person. He wonders if he can get used to the heat.

page 104

The next morning Grandma met them at the airport. Then they drove to the desert. As they hiked, Grandma explained that animals enjoy the open desert space. It gives them the **freedom** to move from place to place. Tim learned that the animals find ways to **adapt** to the hot desert weather. He wondered if he could get used to the desert **climate**.

104

Use Illustrations

The illustrations show me that Tim and his family are visiting a desert. I know that could happen in real life.

Your Turn

COLLABORATE

Give two examples of how you know this story is realistic fiction.

Greg Newbold

110

Prefixes

A prefix is a word part at the beginning of a word. You can separate a prefix, such as *un-* or *dis-*, from the root word.

 Find Text Evidence

I'm not sure what the word unhappy *means. I know that* happy *means to feel good about something. The prefix* un- *means* not. *I think the word means* not happy.

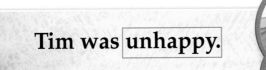

Tim was unhappy.

COLLABORATE

Your Turn

Use prefixes to figure out the meanings of the following words in "A Visit to the Desert."

unlike, page 106
disappeared, *page 105*

Readers to...

Writers share their ideas by including details to describe actions, thoughts, and feelings. Reread the passage from "A Visit to the Desert."

Expert Model

Ideas

Identify two descriptive **details**. How do these details help explain the **ideas**?

Grandma smiled at Tim's excitement. "Actually," she said. "That is a desert tortoise. It looks for shade made by the **shadows** of rocks. That is how it cools off. He burrows underground to get away from the heat."

Greg Newbold

Writers

Ellie wrote a realistic fiction story. Read Ellie's revision.

Editing Marks

∧ Add

⌴ Take out.

⊙ Add a period.

Grammar Handbook

Nouns
See page 477.

Student Model

A Camel at the Zoo

Rosa is on a field trip. ^at the zoo^

She ~~wants~~ is eager to see the camel.

She sees the ^huge, brown^ camel with

a large hump on its back⊙

Rosa is happy to see this

desert animal.

Your Turn

COLLABORATE

- ☑ Identify the details Ellie used.
- ☑ Identify the nouns.
- ☑ Tell how the revisions improved her writing.

Go Digital!
Write online in Writer's Workspace

? Essential Question

What can animals in stories teach us?

Go Digital!

Mircea Catusanu

Animal Lessons

Do you know the story of the Tortoise and the Hare? The Hare is ahead in a race with a slow Tortoise so he decides to take a nap. Then Tortoise ends up winning the race!

▶ Animals in stories teach us lessons.

▶ Animals in stories help us learn about each other.

Talk About It

Talk with a partner about the lessons we learn from animals in stories. Write the lessons on the word web.

Vocabulary

Use the picture and sentence to learn each word.

believe

I **believe** it is going to rain today.

What is something you believe will happen today?

delicious

We ate the **delicious** pizza.

Describe something that tastes delicious.

feast

Our family sat at the dinner table and started to **feast**.

When might you feast?

fond

Rob is very **fond** of his puppy.

What is something that you are fond of?

lessons

I learned a lot from the teacher's **lessons**.

What lessons do you learn at school?

remarkable

I saw a **remarkable** rainbow in the sky.

Describe something that is remarkable.

snatch

My dog can **snatch** a flying disc out of the air.

Show how you would snatch something off your desk.

stories

Our dad reads us **stories** before bedtime.

What are some stories you like?

COLLABORATE

Your Turn

Pick three words. Write three questions for your partner to answer.

Go Digital! *Use the online visual glossary*

(t) amana images inc./Alamy; (tc) Ingram Publishing; (bc) Adrian Sherratt/Alamy; (b) Jupiterimages/BananaStock/Alamy

The Boy
Who Cried
Wolf

Peter Francis

? Essential Question

What can animals in stories teach us?

Read to find out what a shepherd boy learns.

Long ago a shepherd boy sat on a hilltop watching the village sheep. He was not **fond** of his job. He didn't like it one bit. He would have liked something wonderful to happen, but nothing **remarkable** ever did.

The shepherd boy watched the clouds move softly by to stay busy. He saw horses, dogs, and dragons in the sky. He made up **stories** with these things as characters.

Then one day he had a better idea! He took a deep breath and cried out, "Wolf! Wolf! The wolf is chasing the sheep!"

The villagers ran up the hill to help the boy. When they got there, they saw no harmful wolf. The boy laughed. "Shepherd boy! Don't cry 'wolf!' unless there really is a wolf!" said the villagers. They went back down the hill.

Peter Francis

That afternoon the boy again cried out, "Wolf! Wolf! The wolf is chasing the sheep!"

The villagers ran to help the boy again. They saw no wolf. The villagers were angry. "Don't cry 'wolf!' when there is NO WOLF!" they said. The shepherd boy just smiled. The villagers went quickly down the hill again.

That afternoon the boy saw a REAL wolf. He did not want the wolf to grab any of the sheep! The boy thought the wolf would **snatch** one of them for a **delicious**, tasty meal. A sheep would be a big **feast** for a wolf. He quickly jumped to his feet and cried, "WOLF! WOLF!" The villagers thought he was tricking them again, so they did not come.

That night the shepherd boy did not return with their sheep. The villagers found the boy weeping real tears. "There really was a wolf here!" he said. "The flock ran away! When I cried out, 'Wolf! Wolf!' no one came. Why didn't you come?"

A kind man talked to the boy as they walked slowly back to the village. "In the morning, we'll help you look for the sheep," he said. "You have just learned one of life's important **lessons**. This is something you need to know. Nobody **believes** a person who tells lies. It is always better to tell the truth!"

Make Connections

? What did you learn after reading this animal story? ESSENTIAL QUESTION

Tell how you are similar or different from the shepherd boy. TEXT TO SELF

Make Predictions

Use what you read in the story to help you predict, or guess, what might happen next.

Find Text Evidence

On page 120 of "The Boy Who Cried Wolf," I predicted that the boy will upset the villagers.

> **page 121**
>
> That afternoon the boy again cried out, "Wolf! Wolf! The wolf is chasing the sheep!"
>
> The villagers ran to help the boy again. They saw no wolf. The villagers were angry. "Don't cry 'wolf!' when there is NO WOLF!" they said. The shepherd boy just smiled. The villagers went quickly down the hill again.

On page 121, I read that the villagers were angry with the boy. I confirmed my prediction.

Your Turn

When the boy saw the wolf, what did you predict would happen? Point to the place in the text that confirmed your prediction.

Peter Francis

Problem and Solution

The plot is often about the problem in the story. The solution is how the characters solve the problem by the end of the story.

 Find Text Evidence

*In the beginning of "The Boy Who Cried Wolf,"
I read about the boy's problem of being bored.*

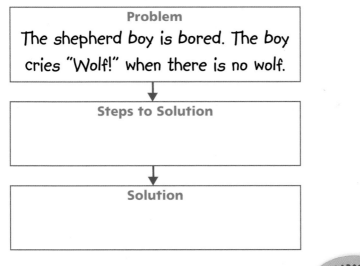

Problem
The shepherd boy is bored. The boy cries "Wolf!" when there is no wolf.

↓

Steps to Solution

↓

Solution

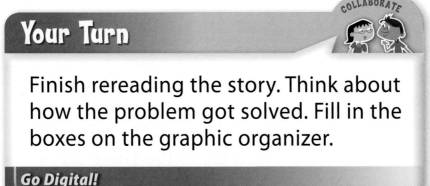

COLLABORATE

Your Turn

Finish rereading the story. Think about how the problem got solved. Fill in the boxes on the graphic organizer.

Go Digital!
Use the interactive graphic organizer

Fable

"The Boy Who Cried Wolf" is a fable. A **fable**:
- is a made-up story that teaches a lesson.
- has a beginning, middle and end.

Find Text Evidence

I can use what I read to tell that "The Boy Who Cried Wolf" is a fable. It is a made-up story that has a beginning, middle, and end.

page 119

Long ago a shepherd boy sat on a hilltop watching the village sheep. He was not **fond** of his job. He didn't like it one bit. He would have liked something wonderful to happen, but nothing **remarkable** ever did.

The shepherd boy watched the clouds move softly by to stay busy. He saw horses, dogs, and dragons in the sky. He made up **stories** with these things as characters.

119

Story Structure

In the **beginning** of the fable, the shepherd boy is bored and plays a trick on the villagers. In the **middle** of the story, the villagers try to teach the boy a lesson.

Your Turn COLLABORATE

Tell how the boy learns a lesson at the **end** of the story.

Suffixes

A suffix is a word part or syllable added to the end of a word. You can separate the root word from a suffix, such as *-ful* or *-ly*, to figure out what the word means.

 Find Text Evidence

I'm not sure what the word harmful *means. The root word is* harm, *which means "to hurt." The suffix is* -ful *which means "full of." I think the word* harmful *means "full of hurt."*

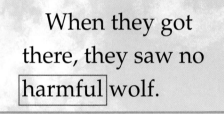

When they got there, they saw no harmful wolf.

 COLLABORATE

Your Turn

Use suffixes to figure out the meanings of these words in "The Boy Who Cried Wolf."
wonderful, *page 119*
softly, *page 119*

Peter Francis

Readers to...

Writers explain their **ideas** by using supporting details. Reread the passage from "The Boy Who Cried Wolf."

Ideas

What **details** does the writer use to help you understand how the villagers feel?

Peter Francis

Expert Model

The Villagers ran to help the boy again. They saw no wolf. The villagers were angry. "Don't cry 'wolf!' when there is NO WOLF!" they said. The shepherd boy just smiled. The villagers went quickly down the hill again.

Writers

Lisa rewrote the beginning of the fable. Read Lisa's revision.

Editing Marks

∧ Add

⊙ Add a period.

ᵧ Take out.

≡ Make a capital letter.

Grammar Handbook

Plural Nouns
See page 479.

Student Model

The Boy Who Cried Wolf

<u>t</u>he shepherd boy was bored.

He was so bored he fell asleep.

He dreamed a wolf came⊙ He

was very scared. He woke

~~woke~~ up and he screamed

"Wolf! There's a wolf running

this way!" The villager^s

came running up the hill.

Your Turn

COLLABORATE

☑ Identify the important details Lisa used.

☑ Identify a plural noun.

☑ Tell how the revisions improved her writing.

Go Digital!
Write online in Writer's Workspace

?

Essential Question

What are features of different animal habitats?

Go Digital!

Animal Homes

Hi! I'm an owl. I live in a special place in nature. I live in a forest habitat. Here's why:

▶ My feathers are the same colors as the trees. This helps me hide from predators.

▶ I can live inside this hole. My babies will be safe.

Talk About It COLLABORATE

Talk with a partner about why animals live in forest habitats. Write your ideas on the web.

Forest Habitat

Vocabulary

Use the picture and sentence to learn each word.

buried

The car was **buried** in the deep snow.

What buried things have you found?

escape

The cat could **escape** through a hole in the fence.

What are other ways an animal could escape from a backyard?

habitat

Prairie dogs live in a desert **habitat**.

What animals live in a forest habitat?

journey

Maya and her family went on a **journey** in the woods.

What is another word for journey?

nature

We walk in the woods because we like to be in **nature**.

What do you like about nature?

peeks

While hiding, Kate **peeks** out from behind the tree.

Show how a person peeks out from behind something.

restless

The child became **restless** during the long car ride.

When have you felt restless?

spies

Carlos **spies** an eagle in the sky.

What is a synonym for spies?

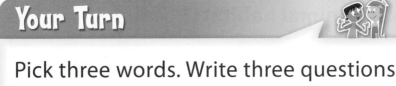

Your Turn

COLLABORATE

Pick three words. Write three questions for your partner to answer.

Go Digital! **Use the online visual glossary**

A Prairie Guard Dog

Essential Question

What are features of different animal habitats?

Read to learn about the place a prairie dog calls home.

Jeff Foott/Getty Images

I am on a **journey**. My trip is to a prairie. It is in the outdoor world called **nature**. Many animals live in a prairie **habitat**. This place has what prairie dogs need to survive. A prairie has a lot of grasses but few trees. Without places to hide, a prairie can be dangerous for some animals.

Good Morning!

It is early in the morning. First, I see a prairie dog. I name him Pete. He **peeks** his head out of his **burrow** underground. He looks around. Then Pete calls loudly to his family, "Yip!" He lets them know it is safe to come out. Soon four prairie dogs come out.

Prairie dogs build underground burrows to keep themselves safe from predators.

Pete is the guard and he is **restless**. He cannot rest because he is always looking around for danger. This allows the other prairie dogs to safely munch on grasses and seeds. They can also groom each other or work on their burrow.

Yap! Yap!

Prairie dogs can make 11 different sounds to communicate with each other.

A Scare

Oh no! Pete **spies** a large badger! When he sees it, he gives a loud bark, "Yap! Yap!" His family recognizes the warning. Some hide in tall grasses, and some jump into the burrow. The badger runs at Pete, but the watchful guard is able to **escape** into the burrow. I am glad he is able to get away from danger.

After a few minutes, Pete peeks his head out again and he is back on the job.

Badgers live on prairies and hunt prairie dogs.

Break Time

The sun gets higher, and it is hot now. The prairie dogs slip into their deep burrow where it is cooler. Even Pete goes in. **Tunnels**, like hallways, lead to different areas. There is a sleeping room. There is a room used like a bathroom. The prairie dogs cover up roots and seeds in one room. Later, they eat the **buried** food there.

Second Shift

I keep watching the burrow. Finally, the sun begins to set and a different prairie dog peeks its head out. I name him Gary. Pete must be off duty. "Yip," Gary calls. The other prairie dogs come back out.

The prairie dogs eat and play until the moon is high in the sky. Then they go to sleep in their burrows. I wonder if Pete will be back on duty. I will see in the morning.

Prairie Dog Facts	
Size	12 to 15 inches tall
Weight	2 to 4 pounds
Habitat	short and medium grass desert prairies
Food	roots, seeds, leaves of plants, grasses
Shelter	underground burrows with many rooms
Predators	coyotes, bobcats, badgers, foxes, weasels

Make Connections

What are two features of a prairie dog's habitat?
ESSENTIAL QUESTION

What animal did the prairie dog remind you of?
TEXT TO SELF

Make Predictions

Use what you already know and what you read in the selection to help you predict what you will learn about. As you read, you can confirm or revise your predictions.

 Find Text Evidence

As I read page 137 of "A Prairie Guard Dog," I predicted that the badger will chase the prairie dog. I read on to see if my prediction was correct.

page 137

A Scare

Oh no! Pete **spies** a large badger! When he sees it, he gives a loud bark, "Yap! Yap!" His family recognizes the warning. Some hide in tall grasses, and some jump into the burrow. The badger runs at Pete, but the watchful guard is able to **escape** into the burrow. I am glad he is able to get away from danger.

On page 137, I read that the badger ran at Pete. My prediction was correct.

COLLABORATE

Your Turn

Reread page 138. What did you predict would happen next? Look for text clues to decide if your prediction was correct.

Main Topic and Key Details

The main topic is what the selection is about. Key details give information about the main topic.

 Find Text Evidence

As I read "A Prairie Guard Dog," I learn a lot about prairie dogs. This must be the main topic. On page 135, I learn a key detail about prairie dogs.

Main Topic		
Prairie Dogs		
Key Detail	**Key Detail**	**Key Detail**
A prairie dog acts as a guard.		

Your Turn

COLLABORATE

Continue rereading the story. Fill in key details about the main topic on the graphic organizer.

Go Digital!
Use the interactive graphic organizer

Narrative Nonfiction

"A Prairie Guard Dog" is narrative nonfiction.
A **Narrative Nonfiction**:

- tells about living things, people, or events.
- is told by a narrator and follows a sequence.

Find Text Evidence

I can use what I read to tell that "A Prairie Guard Dog" is a narrative nonfiction. A narrator tells the story about what real prairie dogs do.

page 138

Break Time

The sun gets higher, and it is hot now. The prairie dogs slip into their deep burrow where it is cooler. Even Pete goes in. **Tunnels**, like hallways, lead to different areas. There is a sleeping room. There is a room used like a bathroom. The prairie dogs cover up roots and seeds in one room. Later, they eat the **buried** food there.

138

Text Features

Headings Headings tell what a section of text is mostly about.

Bold Print These words are important to understanding the text.

Your Turn

Identify text features on a different page. Tell what information you learned from these features.

Suffixes

A suffix is a word part or syllable added to the end of a word. You can separate the root word from a suffix, such as *-ful* or *-ly*, to figure out what the word means.

 Find Text Evidence

I'm not sure what the word loudly *means. The root word is* loud, *which means "full of noise." The suffix is* -ly *which means "in a certain way." I think the word* loudly *means "in a noisy way."*

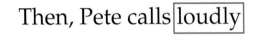

Then, Pete calls loudly to his family, "Yip!"

COLLABORATE

Your Turn

Use suffixes to figure out the meanings of these words in "A Prairie Guard Dog."
safely, *page 136*
watchful, *page 137*
finally, *page 139*

Corbis Flirt/Alamy

Readers to...

Writers use sequence to put their ideas in an order. Words, such as *first, next,* and *then* help readers understand the order of the ideas.

Organization
Identify the **sequence** words. How does this help the **organization** of the story?

Jeff Foott/Getty Images

Expert Model

Good Morning!

It is early in the morning. First, I see a prairie dog. I name him Pete. He peeks his head out of his burrow underground. He looks around. Then Pete calls loudly to his family, "Yip!" He lets them know it is safe to come out. Soon four prairie dogs come out.

Writers

Adam wrote a nonfiction story about a seal. Read Adam's revision.

Grammar Handbook

Kinds of Nouns
See page 477–478.

Student Model

Sam Learns to Swim

At two weeks old, s̲am Seal has his first swimming lesson. His mother guides him into the water. ~~He is two weeks old.~~ ∧At first He does not want to go in. He gets out and shakes his head. Then Mom guides him back in. He flaps his flippers. Finally, he is learning!

Your Turn
COLLABORATE

- ☑ Point out the sequence words Adam used.
- ☑ Identify the proper nouns.
- ☑ Tell how revisions improved his writing.

Go Digital!
Write online in Writer's Workspace

? Essential Question

How are offspring like their parents?

Go Digital!

Animal
Babies and Parents

This baby penguin and his mother look different but they are the same in many ways.

▶ They both have layers of fat to keep warm.

▶ They are both birds, not mammals.

▶ They both use their flippers to swim.

Talk About It

COLLABORATE

Talk with a partner about how baby penguins are the same as and different from their parents. Write your ideas on the chart.

Same	Different

Vocabulary

Use the picture and sentence to learn each word.

adult

My father is an **adult**.

What is the opposite of an adult?

alive

I water the flowers to keep them **alive**.

How can you tell that a plant is alive?

covered

Polar bears are **covered** with thick, white fur.

What are birds covered with?

fur

My kitten has **fur** that is soft and fluffy.

What are some other animals that have fur?

giant

That **giant** tree is taller than my house.

Tell about the most giant thing you have ever seen.

groom

I use a brush to **groom** my horse each day.

What is another word for groom?

mammal

A **mammal** has fur or hair and breathes air.

Describe a mammal you know about.

offspring

At the zoo, we saw a mother rabbit and two **offspring**.

What is the name for the offspring of a dog?

Your Turn

COLLABORATE

Pick three words. Write three questions for your partner to answer.

Go Digital! **Use the online visual glossary**

Eagles and Eaglets

Essential Question

How are offspring like their parents?

Read to learn how young bald eagles are like their parents.

Bald eagles are birds. The baby birds, or **offspring** are called eaglets. Let's read about how eaglets are like their parents.

It's Nesting Time

All birds lay eggs. Bald eagles build their nests in the tops of trees so the eggs will be safe. Their nests are built of sticks and grass. They add on to their nests each year. They can become huge! These **giant** nests can be as large as nine feet across. That's bigger than your bed!

The mother eagle lays from one to three eggs. She sits on her eggs until they hatch. Then both parents watch over the nest.

Proud Parents

At first the eaglets are helpless. They cannot walk. They need their parents for food. They also cannot see well. Birds are not **mammals**. They do not have milk to feed their young. They hunt for food. Eaglets also need their parents for safety.

Eaglets Grow Up

Bald eagles use their sharp eyes to hunt. They use their strong wings to fly fast. They also use their claws and beak to catch fish. Young eaglets must learn all these things. Then they can live on their own.

The eagles must bring food to the eaglets.

Unlike mammals, birds have feathers, not **fur**. An eaglet is born **covered** with soft gray down. It cannot fly until it grows dark feathers like its parents. The eaglet stays near the nest until its wings grow strong. That takes about five months.

Bald Eagle

powerful eyes

hooked yellow beak

dark feathers on body and wings

white tail feathers

long claws

Frank Leung/Getty Images

An eaglet becomes an **adult** when it has learned to do all the things its parents do. This takes about five years. Bald eagles can stay **alive** for up to thirty years.

When the bald eagle soars, the feathers on its huge wings spread out like fingers.

Bald Eagles Soar

Once it learns to fly, the bald eagle can soar for hours. The bald eagle must take good care of its feathers. It uses its beak to **groom** itself. It must keep its feathers clean. Can you believe this powerful eagle began life as a helpless baby?

Make Connections

How is the eaglet like its parents? How is it different? **ESSENTIAL QUESTION**

Compare how your parents and eagle parents take care of their young. **TEXT TO SELF**

Reread

As you read, you may come across new words or information you don't understand. You can reread to help you understand the text.

Find Text Evidence

On page 152 of "Eagles and Eaglets," the text tells how birds are helpless. I will go back and reread to understand how they are helpless.

page 152

Proud Parents

At first the eaglets are helpless. They cannot walk. They need their parents for food. They also cannot see well. Birds are not **mammals**. They do not have milk to feed their young. They hunt for food. Eaglets also need their parents for safety.

Eaglets Grow Up

Bald eagles use their sharp eyes to hunt. They use their strong wings to fly fast.

I read that eaglets cannot walk so they need their parents to get them food. This explains how they are helpless.

COLLABORATE

Your Turn

Why are eagles not able to fly when they are born? Reread page 153 to help you answer the question.

Accent Alaska.com/Alamy

Main Topic and Key Details

The main topic is what the selection is about. Key details give information about the main topic.

 Find Text Evidence

As I read page 151 I learn a lot about eagles. This must be the main topic. I also read details about eagles.

Main Topic Eagles		
Key Detail Eagles build nests and lay eggs.	**Key Detail**	**Key Detail**

Your Turn

Continue reading the story. Fill in the graphic organizer with more key details that tell about the topic.

Go Digital!
Use the interactive graphic organizer

Expository Text

The selection "Eagles and Eaglets" is an expository text. An **Expository text**:
- gives facts about a topic.
- can have text features.

🔍 Find Text Evidence

I know that "Eagles and Eaglets" is an expository text because it gives facts about eagles. It also has text features that help me learn about eagles.

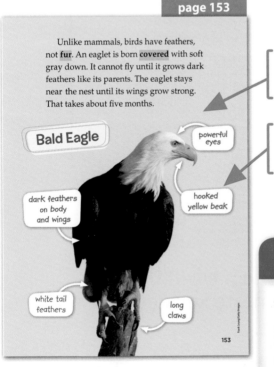

page 153

Unlike mammals, birds have feathers, not **fur**. An eaglet is born **covered** with soft gray down. It cannot fly until it grows dark feathers like its parents. The eaglet stays near the nest until its wings grow strong. That takes about five months.

Bald Eagle

powerful eyes

dark feathers on body and wings

hooked yellow beak

white tail feathers

long claws

153

Text Features

A **diagram** is a picture that shows information.

The **labels** explain the parts of the diagram.

Your Turn

COLLABORATE

Tell what information you learned from looking at the diagram and reading the labels.

Multiple-Meaning Words

Multiple-meaning words have more than one meaning. Use the other words in a sentence to figure out which meaning is being used.

Find Text Evidence

I'm not sure what the word add *means. This word could mean "to put on something extra," or it could mean "to put numbers together." Since the eagles are making a nest, I think the first meaning makes sense in this sentence.*

They add on to their nests each year.

Your Turn

COLLABORATE

Use sentence clues to figure out the meanings of these words in "Eagles and Eaglets."
   watch, *page 151*
   fly, *page 152*

Takayuki Maekawa/Getty Images

Readers to...

Writers choose linking words to show how ideas in a story are related. Some linking words are *and, so*, and *also*. Reread the section from "Eagles and Eaglets" below.

Expert Model

Word Choice

Identify two **linking words**. How do these words help you understand the selection?

It's Nesting Time

All birds lay eggs. Bald eagles build their nests in the tops of trees so the eggs will be safe. Their nests are built of sticks and grass. They add on to their nests each year. They can become huge! These **giant** nests can be as large as nine feet across. That's bigger than your bed!

Louis Gagnon/naturepl.com

Writers

Robert wrote an expository text.
Read Robert's revision.

Editing Marks

≡ Make a capital letter.

∧ Add

✗ Take out.

(sp) Check spelling.

Grammar Handbook

Plural Nouns
See page 479.

Student Model

fawns
≡

A mother deer's baby is

fawn   (sp) mammals
called a baby. Deer are mamals.
        ∧

The mother gives milk to the

fawn and keeps it hidden. Later,

the fawn follows the mother and

looks for plants. Soon the young

deer can be on

its own.

Your Turn

COLLABORATE

☑ Identify the linking words Robert used.
☑ Identify a plural noun.
☑ Tell how revisions improved his writing.

Go Digital!
Write online in Writer's Workspace

? Essential Question

What do we love about animals?

Go Digital!

Animal Fun

Animals are fun to play with. This dolphin is large, wet, and makes whistling sounds. We can use sensory words to describe animals.

▶ We can describe how an animal looks, feels, sounds, and smells.

▶ We can tell how animals behave and express themselves.

Talk About It

COLLABORATE

Use sensory words to talk with a partner about an animal you like. Write your ideas on the web.

Words That Describe a _____.

Vocabulary

Use the picture and sentence to learn each word.

behave

The boy is teaching the dog to **behave**.

How do you *behave* when you are in the library?

flapping

The bird was **flapping** its wings quickly.

Describe what flapping is.

express

This baby is smiling to **express** how he feels.

How do you express your feelings?

feathers

A peacock is covered in colorful **feathers**.

Where else have you seen feathers?

Poetry Words

poem

A **poem** is a form of writing that expresses imagination or feelings.

How is a poem different from a story?

rhyme

When two words **rhyme**, they have the same ending sounds.

What words could a poet use to rhyme with cat?

rhythm

Rhythm is the repeating accents, or beats, in a poem.

Why would a poet want a poem to have rhythm?

word choice

Word choice is the use of rich, colorful, exact words.

What exact word could you use to describe how you feel right now?

COLLABORATE

Your Turn

Pick three words and write a question about each for your partner to answer.

Go Digital! **Use the online visual glossary**

Cats and Kittens

?

Essential Question

What do we love about animals?

Read how poets describe animals they love.

Cats and kittens **express** their views
With hisses, purrs, and little mews.

Instead of taking baths like me,
They use their tongues quite handily.

I wonder what my mom would say
If I tried cleaning up that way.

They stay as still as still can be,
Until a mouse they chance to see.

And then in one great flash of fur
They pounce on a toy with a PURRRR.

— by Constance Keremes

Desert Camels

Camels have a hump on their backs
To carry people and their sacks.

They're very strong, don't mind the Sun,
Won't stop for drinks until they're done.

They give people a bouncy ride.
They sway and move from side to side.

I'd like a camel for a pet,
But haven't asked my mother yet!

— by Martine Wren

A Bat Is Not a Bird

A bat has neither **feathers** nor beak.
He does not chirp, just gives a shriek.

He flies by hearing sounds like pings,
Flapping, flapping his leathery wings.

At night when I'm asleep in my bed,
He gets to fly around instead!

— **by Trevor Reynolds**

Make Connections

Talk about what the poet loves about the animal in each poem. **ESSENTIAL QUESTION**

Describe how your favorite animal **behaves**. **TEXT TO SELF**

Photri Images/Alamy

Rhyming Poem

A **rhyming poem**:
- has words that end with the same sounds.
- tells a poet's thoughts or feelings.

🔍 **Find Text Evidence**

I can tell that "Cats and Kittens" is a rhyming poem. The author tells her thoughts about cats. Also, the last words in lines one and two rhyme.

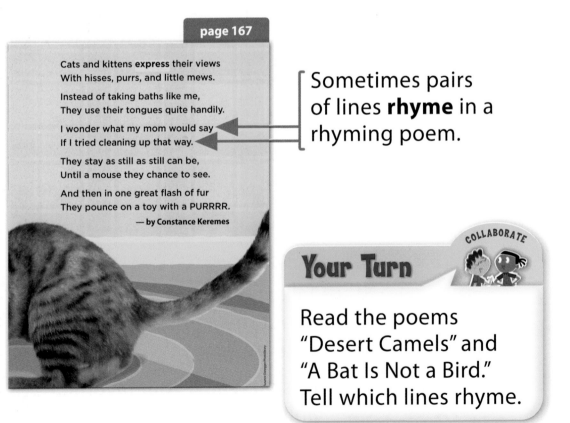

page 167

Cats and kittens **express** their views
With hisses, purrs, and little mews.

Instead of taking baths like me,
They use their tongues quite handily.

I wonder what my mom would say
If I tried cleaning up that way.

They stay as still as still can be,
Until a mouse they chance to see.

And then in one great flash of fur
They pounce on a toy with a PURRRR.

— by Constance Keremes

Sometimes pairs of lines **rhyme** in a rhyming poem.

Your Turn COLLABORATE

Read the poems "Desert Camels" and "A Bat Is Not a Bird." Tell which lines rhyme.

Key Details

Key details give important information about a poem. You can find important information in the words, pictures, or photos.

 Find Text Evidence

As I read "Desert Camels," I understand that camels are very strong. I read that they can carry people and their sacks.

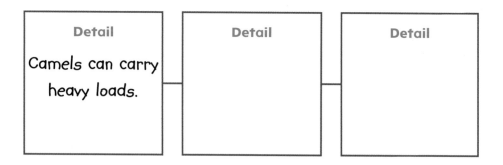

Detail	Detail	Detail
Camels can carry heavy loads.		

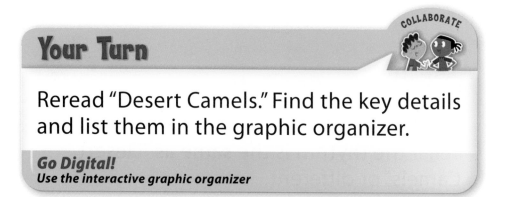

COLLABORATE

Your Turn

Reread "Desert Camels." Find the key details and list them in the graphic organizer.

Go Digital!
Use the interactive graphic organizer

171

Rhythm

Poems have rhythm. Rhythm is the repeating accents in a poem. You can clap the rhythm, or beats, in a poem.

Find Text Evidence

Reread "Desert Camels," and listen to the rhythm. Listen to the beats in each line. Think about why the poet uses rhythm.

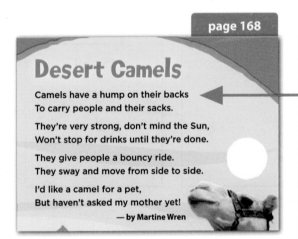

page 168

Desert Camels

Camels have a hump on their backs
To carry people and their sacks.

They're very strong, don't mind the Sun,
Won't stop for drinks until they're done.

They give people a bouncy ride.
They sway and move from side to side.

I'd like a camel for a pet,
But haven't asked my mother yet!

— by Martine Wren

I clap the beats in the first line. There are eight beats. There are also eight beats in the second line. The beats make the poem fun to read.

COLLABORATE

Your Turn

Clap the first two lines of "Cats and Kittens." Tell if the rhythm is the same as "Desert Camels" or different.

Tom Schwabel/Flickr/Getty Images

Multiple-Meaning Words

Multiple-meaning words are words that are spelled the same but have more than one meaning. You can use context clues to help you understand the correct meaning.

Find Text Evidence

In "A Bat Is Not a Bird," I see the word bat. *I know a bat is an animal and also something you use to play baseball. The words "feathers" and "beak" tell me the author is talking about an animal.*

page 169

A **bat** has neither feathers nor beak.

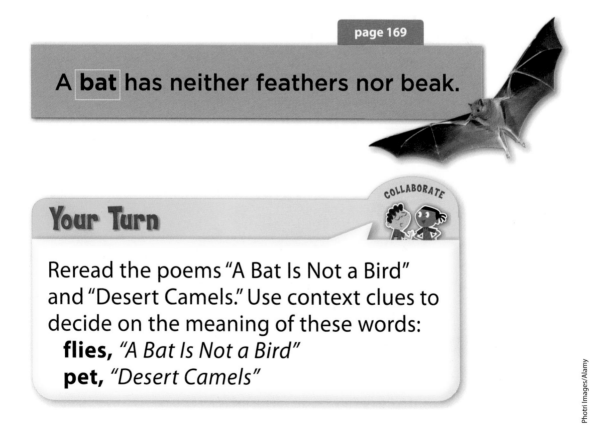

COLLABORATE

Your Turn

Reread the poems "A Bat Is Not a Bird" and "Desert Camels." Use context clues to decide on the meaning of these words:
    flies, *"A Bat Is Not a Bird"*
    pet, *"Desert Camels"*

Photri Images/Alamy

173

Readers to . . .

Writers use precise words to tell exactly what they mean so readers form a clear picture in their minds. Reread "Cats and Kittens" below.

Word Choice
Identify a **precise word** the writer uses. How does this word help you understand how cats act?

Cats and kittens express their
    views
With hisses, purrs, and little
    mews.

Instead of taking baths like
    me,
They use their tongues quite
    handily.

Writers

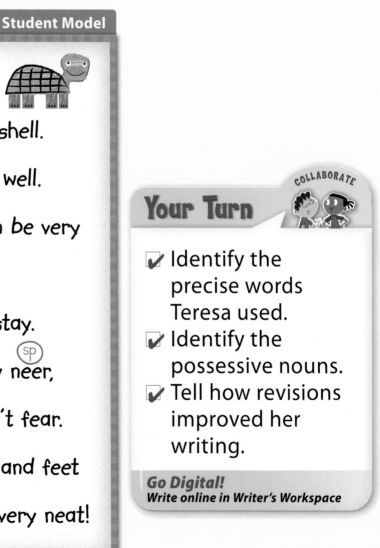

Teresa wrote a poem. Read Teresa's revisions.

Editing Marks

(sp) Check spelling.

∧ Add.

✗ Take out.

Grammar Handbook

Possessive Nouns
See page 480.

Student Model

A Turtle

A turtle has a hard shell.

It fits him very very well.

The turtle's shell can be very gray.

It's a nice ^{safe}∧ place to stay.

When danger is very neer, (sp)

The shy turtle doesn't fear.

He pulls in his head and feet

And he's gone. How very neat!

Your Turn   COLLABORATE

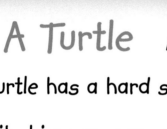

- ☑ Identify the precise words Teresa used.
- ☑ Identify the possessive nouns.
- ☑ Tell how revisions improved her writing.

Go Digital!
Write online in Writer's Workspace

175

Live and Learn

The Big Idea

What have you learned about
the world that surprises you?

Patricia Castelao

Surprises, Surprises

Our world is a jumble of land, sky, and sea,
Surprises, surprises are all around me.

Boats float on water, balloons float on air,
Surprises, surprises are everywhere.

A lamp gives us light, and so does the Sun,
Surprises, surprises for everyone.

We're all different sizes—round, thin, short, or tall,
Surprises, surprises—some giant, some small.

Summer brings sunshine, the winter brings snow,
I see surprises wherever I go.

Friends can be next door or far away too,
Surprises, surprises for me and for you.

by Maureen Wong

? **Essential Question**

How do the Earth's forces affect us?

Go Digital!

The Earth Affects Us

Down, down, down you go! Gravity is the force that pulls you down the slide. Here are some other ways you can see the force of gravity at work.

▶ A ball rolling and picking up speed.

▶ A child jumping.

Talk About It

Talk with a partner about ways you can see gravity at work. Then write your ideas on the web.

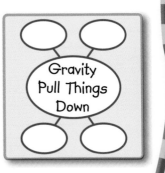

Gravity Pull Things Down

Vocabulary

Use the picture and sentence to learn each word.

amazing

Jason made an **amazing** flip into the pool.

What have you seen that is amazing to you?

force

The **force** of my kick made the ball move far.

What things take a lot of force to move?

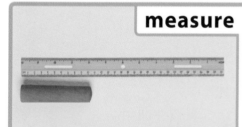

measure

I can **measure** the chalk with my ruler.

What other tool can you use to measure things?

objects

There were lots of **objects** in the toy chest.

Tell about the biggest object you have seen that is a toy.

proved

Wyatt's big hit **proved** he knew how to play baseball.

What is a way you have proved something?

speed

The car moved at a very fast **speed**.

What are some things that move at a slow speed?

true

It is **true** that an elephant is the largest land animal.

What is the opposite of true?

weight

The **weight** of the pumpkin made it heavy to carry.

What can you do to find the weight of something?

Your Turn

COLLABORATE

Pick three words. Write three questions for your partner to answer.

Go Digital! *Use the online visual glossary*

Magnets Work!

? Essential Question

How do the earth's forces affect us?

Read to learn about magnets and how they help us.

Did you know magnets are all around you? Magnets help you do **amazing** things! Keep reading! See if you think magnets have surprising uses.

Magnets Pull

Look closely and you will see. Magnets can be found on a can opener. The magnet **attracts,** or pulls, the lid off of a soup can. A push or pull is called a **force**.

There is also a magnet in a refrigerator. It pulls the metal in the door to make a tight seal. Do you know how?

A magnet's force pulls **objects** made of metals called iron and steel. It will not pull other things. It will not pull a wooden pencil or a plastic toy. A magnet does not attract all items.

Magnets Have Poles

You have **proved**, or shown, that magnets can pull some things to it. Why is this true? The two ends of a magnet are its **poles**. Every magnet has a north pole and a south pole.

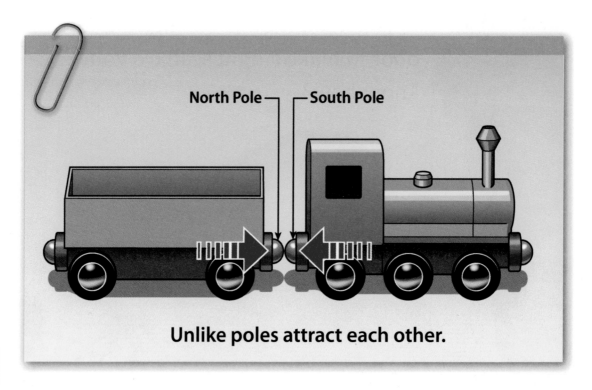

North Pole — — South Pole

Unlike poles attract each other.

Steve Schell

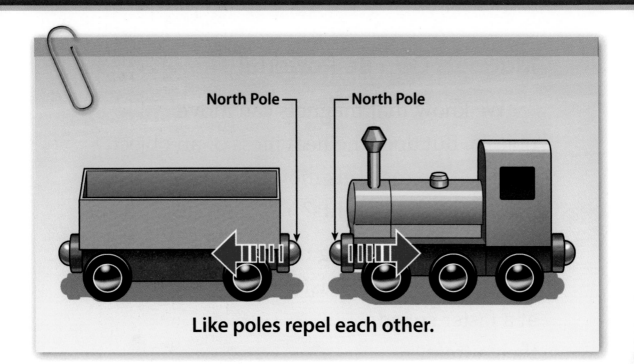

North Pole **North Pole**

Like poles repel each other.

Have you ever played with trains that have magnets? Sometimes, you try to put two train cars together, but they **repel.** This means they push away from each other.

Then you turn one of the cars around. The two cars snap together as quick as a wink. That's right! If you have played with these trains, you know it is **true.**

When the train cars push away, two of the same poles are facing each other. However, if you put the north and south poles together, they will snap together like the train.

Magnets Can Be Powerful

We know that magnets can move objects. But does the heaviness of an object matter? Can magnets move objects that have different **weights**? Yes, they can.

Scientists are using magnets in new ways. People often wish they could travel at a faster **speed** than a train.

The magnets on this train make it float over the track.

There is a new train that uses powerful magnets to travel more quickly. Magnets lift the train above the track and push the train forward. The train appears to be moving as fast as lightning! Scientists have **measured** these train speeds. They are much faster than the trains we know.

Can you imagine what magnets will help us do in the future?

Make Connections

What are two ways we use magnets? ESSENTIAL QUESTION

Tell about a time when you have used a magnet to push or pull something. TEXT TO SELF

Reread

As you read, you may come across words, facts, or explanations that are new to you. Reread these parts to make sure you understand them.

Find Text Evidence

After reading page 184 of "Magnets Work!", I am not sure why magnets don't pull objects made of wood. I will reread to figure out why.

> **page 184**
>
> A magnet's force pulls **objects** made of metals called iron and steel. It will not pull other things. It will not pull a wooden pencil or a plastic toy. A magnet does not attract all items.
>
> **Magnets Have Poles**
>
> You have **proved**, or shown, that magnets can pull some things to it. Why is

I reread the page and understand now that a magnet's force only pulls objects made of iron and steel.

 **Your Turn**

COLLABORATE

Reread pages 184 and 185. Explain why magnets sometimes push away from each other.

Author's Purpose

Authors write to tell information, explain, or describe. As you read, look for clues to the author's purpose.

Find Text Evidence

As I reread page 183 of "Magnets Work!", I found how magnets are used. I think this is a clue about what the author's purpose may be.

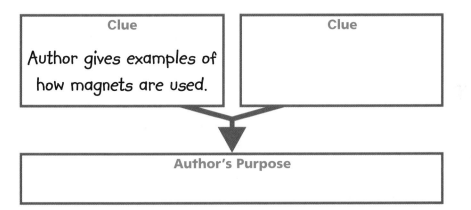

Clue	Clue
Author gives examples of how magnets are used.	

Author's Purpose

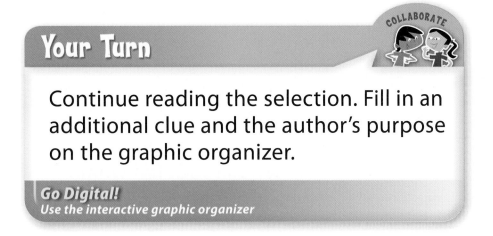

Your Turn

COLLABORATE

Continue reading the selection. Fill in an additional clue and the author's purpose on the graphic organizer.

Go Digital!
Use the interactive graphic organizer

Expository Text

"Magnets Work!" is an expository text.
Expository text:
- gives information about a topic.
- can include text features.

Find Text Evidence

I know that "Magnets Work!" is an expository text because it explains facts about magnets.

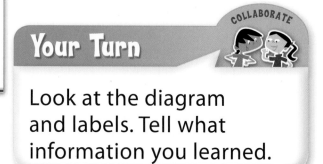

page 184

A magnet's force pulls **objects** made of metals called iron and steel. It will not pull other things. It will not pull a wooden pencil or a plastic toy. A magnet does not attract all items.

Magnets Have Poles

You have **proved**, or shown, that magnets can pull some things to it. Why is this true? The two ends of a magnet are its **poles**. Every magnet has a north pole and a south pole.

North Pole — South Pole

Unlike poles attract each other.

184

Text Features

Subheadings tell you what a section of text is mostly about.

Diagrams help you understand how something works.

COLLABORATE

Your Turn

Look at the diagram and labels. Tell what information you learned.

Similes

A simile uses the word *like* or *as* to compare two different things. To understand a simile, figure out how an author compares one thing to another.

 Find Text Evidence

I see the word as *in the sentence, "The two cars snap together as quick as a wink." I know the author is comparing how fast two train cars hook together with how fast a person blinks.*

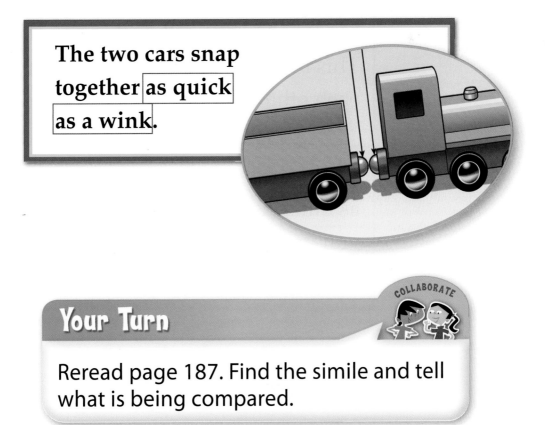

The two cars snap together as quick as a wink.

Your Turn

COLLABORATE

Reread page 187. Find the simile and tell what is being compared.

Steve Schell.

191

Readers to...

Writers put their ideas in an order that makes sense to readers. Reread the passage from "Magnets Work!"

Expert Model

Organization
How did the author **order** her **ideas?**

Have you ever played with trains that have magnets? Sometimes, you try to put two train cars together, but they **repel**. This means they push away from each other.

Then you turn one of the cars around. The two cars snap together as quick as a wink. That's right! If you have played with these trains, you know it is true.

Steve Schell

Writers

Carlos wrote an expository text. Read Carlos's writing.

Editing Marks

/ Make a small letter.

^ Add

ℐ Take out.

Grammar Handbook

Action Verbs
See page 481.

Student Model

Basketball Pushes and Pulls

You push and pull when you
~~do~~ basketball. When you dribble
play ^

the ball, your hand pushes

the ball down to the ground.
Also, ^

When you shoot the ball, you

push it away from you. Then,

If someone takes the ball from

you, she uses a pull. She

pulls the ball to her.

Your Turn

COLLABORATE

- ☑ Identify how Carlos ordered his ideas.
- ☑ Identify the action verbs.
- ☑ Tell how revisions improved his writing.

Go Digital!
Write online in Writer's Workspace

Essential Question

What can we see in the sky?

Go Digital!

Up in the Sky

When you are outside, what do you see in the sky?

▶ The sky and clouds

▶ The moon

▶ A rainbow

Talk About It COLLABORATE

Talk with a partner about what you see in the daytime and nighttime skies. List these features on the chart.

Daytime Sky	Nighttime Sky
sunlight	moonlight

CCSS **Words to Know**

Vocabulary

Use the picture and sentence to learn each word.

adventure

I want to travel around the world and find **adventure**.

Where might you go to find adventure?

delighted

Ling was **delighted** when her grandmother came to visit.

What makes you feel delighted?

dreamed

Juan **dreamed** of being an actor when he grows up.

What is something you have dreamed about?

enjoyed

We **enjoyed** playing in the pool on the hot day.

What is another word for enjoyed?

(t) Lane Oatey/blue jean images/Getty Images; (tc) Tom Merton/OJO Images/Getty Images; (bc) ColorBlind Images/Blend Images/Getty Images; (b) Ingram Publishing/SuperStock

grumbled

My stomach **grumbled** because I was hungry.

Name something that makes a grumbling sound.

moonlight

Moonlight can help sailors see at night.

What else can moonlight help you do?

neighbor

I went across the street to play with my **neighbor**.

Tell about a neighbor you have.

nighttime

I like to watch the stars at **nighttime**.

What is the opposite of nighttime?

Your Turn

COLLABORATE

Pick three words. Write three questions for your partner to answer.

Go Digital! **Use the online visual glossary**

Starry Night

Essential Question

What can we see in the sky?

Read about what happens when two girls look for the Big Dipper.

Chris Canga

Josie and Ling were good friends. Ling was happy Josie was her **neighbor**. Josie was happy Ling lived nearby, too.

Josie and Ling couldn't wait for the school day to end. They planned a sleepover at Josie's house. They were going to sleep in a tent in Josie's backyard.

As the class was leaving, Mr. Cortes said, "Your weekend homework is to look at the **nighttime** sky and explain what you saw on Monday." The class **grumbled**. "Why the unhappy sounds?" Mr. Cortes asked. "It will be fun looking at the sky at night."

The girls arrived at Josie's house and were **delighted** to be sleeping outdoors. Josie said, "I'm so happy that we get to sleep in the tent. It will be lots of fun." Then Ling said, "I'll get the sleeping bags and flashlights. I brought flashlights so we can play games in the tent."

Josie's dad poked his head inside the tent. "Girls, it is a good time to do your homework now because it is getting dark," he said. "Awww," they both complained. "Dad," said Josie, "do we have to, now?"

"Yes, I already set up the telescope."

Chris Canga

Ling said, "I hope this won't take too long." Josie looked up and spotted a crescent moon. "Did you know the moon's light comes from the sun?" said Josie. "It's funny that it's called **moonlight**." "Yes," said Ling, who was still thinking about playing in the tent.

Josie's dad smiled at the girls and said, "See the stars in the sky? Those points of bright light can form shapes."

The Big Dipper

"You can see the Big Dipper," he said. "It's a group of stars that look like a giant spoon in the sky."

Josie's dad showed her how to look through the telescope. "Wow, that's more stars than I ever **dreamed** of. I never imagined there could be so many."

It was Ling's turn to look. Ling cried out, "I see a bright light moving in the sky!"

"That's a shooting star!" said Josie's dad.

"This is fun," said Ling. "I really **enjoy** looking at the stars."

Chris Canga

"I think we've seen enough of the nighttime sky," said Josie's dad. "You girls can go play now."

"Aw, Dad, can't we keep looking?" asked Josie. "This is really fun."

"Yes," said Ling. "We have had an **adventure** already, and we haven't even played in the tent yet!"

"You're right, Ling," said Josie. "This has been one exciting night."

Make Connections

What did you learn about the nighttime sky after reading this story? ESSENTIAL QUESTION

Compare what the girls saw in the nighttime sky to what you have seen in the nighttime sky. TEXT TO SELF

Reread

As you read, you can stop and reread the parts you do not understand or may have missed. This will help you understand what you read.

Find Text Evidence

On page 201 of "Starry Night," I am not sure what the Big Dipper is. I will reread this part of the story to see if I missed anything.

page 201

long." Josie looked up and spotted a crescent moon. "Did you know the moon's light comes from the sun?" said Josie. "It's funny that it's called **moonlight**." "Yes," said Ling, who was still thinking about playing in the tent.

Josie's dad smiled at the girls and said, "See the stars in the sky? Those points of bright light can form shapes."

"You can see the Big Dipper," he said. "It's a group of stars that look like a giant spoon in the sky."

The Big Dipper

201

I read that the Big Dipper is a group of stars that look like a giant spoon in the sky.

Your Turn

COLLABORATE

What does a telescope help you do? Reread page 202 to answer the question.

Sequence

The sequence tells the order of events in the story. We can use the words *first*, *next*, *then* and *last* to tell the order of what happens.

Find Text Evidence

As I read page 199 of "Starry Night," I think about the sequence in the story.

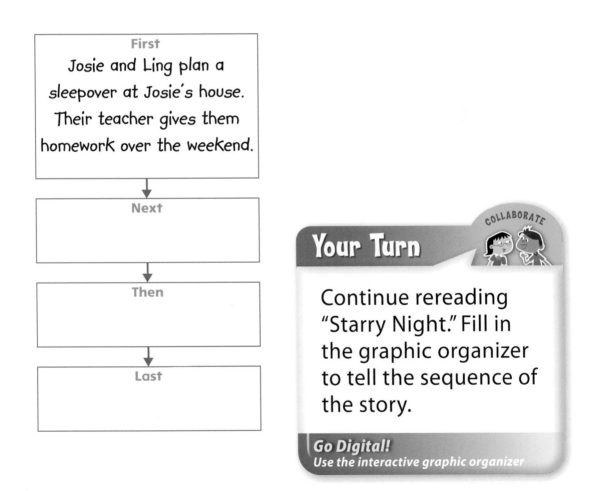

First
Josie and Ling plan a sleepover at Josie's house. Their teacher gives them homework over the weekend.

↓

Next

↓

Then

↓

Last

Your Turn COLLABORATE

Continue rereading "Starry Night." Fill in the graphic organizer to tell the sequence of the story.

Go Digital!
Use the interactive graphic organizer

Fiction

The story "Starry Night" is fiction.
Fiction:
- has made-up characters and events.
- has dialogue.

Find Text Evidence

I can use what I read to tell that "Starry Night" is fiction. The characters are made up and they talk to each other.

page 199

Josie and Ling were good friends. Ling was happy Josie was her **neighbor**. Josie was happy Ling lived nearby, too.

Josie and Ling couldn't wait for the school day to end. They planned a sleepover at Josie's house. They were going to sleep in a tent in Josie's backyard.

As the class was leaving, Mr. Cortes said, "Your weekend homework is to look at the **nighttime** sky and explain what you saw on Monday." The class **grumbled**. "Why the unhappy sounds?" Mr. Cortes asked. "It will be fun looking at the sky at night."

199

Story Structure
Dialogue is when characters in a story talk to each other.

Your Turn

Identify other places in the story that tell you the story is fiction.

Compound Words

A compound word is made of two smaller words. Think of the meanings of the smaller words to figure out the meaning of the compound word.

Find Text Evidence

I see the word sleepover. *The first part of this word is* sleep, *which means "to close your eyes and rest." The second part of this word is* over, *which can mean "at another place." I think* sleepover *means "sleeping at someone's house."*

> "They planned a | sleepover |
> at Josie's house."

COLLABORATE

Your Turn

Use the meanings of the smaller words to figure out the meanings of these compound words in "Starry Night."
 homework, *page 199*
 backyard, *page 199*

Chris Canga

Readers to . . .

Writers choose linking words to show how their ideas are connected. Linking words can show how ideas work together.

Word Choice
Identify two **linking words**. Tell how these ideas in the story are connected.

Then Ling said, "I'll get the sleeping bags and flashlights. I brought flashlights so we can play games in the tent."

Josie's dad poked his head inside the tent. "Girls, it is a good time to do your homework now because it is getting dark," he said. "Awww," they both complained. "Dad" said Josie, "do we have to, now?" "Yes, I already set up the telescope."

Chris Canga

Writers

Editing Marks

⊙ Add a period.

∧ Add

✐ Take out.

Grammar Handbook

Present-Tense Verbs See page 482.

Derek wrote a fiction story about camping. Read Derek's story.

Student Model

Watching the Stars

James and Dad were camping⊙

There was not much moonlight

but there were a lot of stars

James
out. He said, "I see the Big

Dipper." James dreamed he

so
took a rocket ship,

he could see

more stars.

Your Turn COLLABORATE

- ☑ Identify the linking words Derek used.
- ☑ Identify a present-tense verb.
- ☑ Tell how the revisions improved his writing.

Go Digital!
Write online in Writer's Workspace

Essential Question

How can people help out their community?

Go Digital!

SuperStudio/The Image Bank/Getty Images

Let's Help Out!

This garden was once an empty lot filled with garbage. A few neighbors thought of a solution to this problem. Their idea was to make a garden.

▶ We cleaned up the lot.

▶ We planted flowers and plants.

Talk About It

Work with a partner. Think of some ways you can help out in your community. Write your ideas on the word web.

Ways to Help Out

Vocabulary

Use the picture and sentence to learn each word.

across

We walked **across** the street.

Tell about something else you might walk across.

borrow

I like to **borrow** books from the library in my town.

What are some things you might borrow?

countryside

The quiet **countryside** is full of grass and trees.

Tell about some other things you might find in the countryside.

idea

Kate had an **idea** for how to make a paper crane.

Name an idea you have for a game to play.

insists

Mom **insists** we wear our seatbelts.

What is something your teacher insists on?

lonely

Gabe was **lonely** when his friend moved away.

When have you felt lonely?

solution

Dylan found a **solution** for his problem.

What is a solution for spilled milk?

villages

Few people live in the small **villages** on the mountain.

Tell what you might see in small villages.

Your Turn

COLLABORATE

Pick three words. Write three questions for your partner to answer.

Go Digital! **Use the online visual glossary**

Lighting Lives

? Essential Question

How can people help out their community?

Read to learn how one person is helping people in her community.

When Debby Tewa was your age, her home had no electricity. She could not flip a light switch to read at night. She lit a candle. She could not cook on a stove or in a microwave oven. Her family cooked over a fire.

Debby lived in Arizona. When she was ten, she moved to a new home. Her new home had electricity! She could turn on a lamp and use a phone. She liked it!

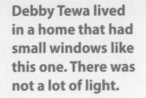

Debby Tewa lived in a home that had small windows like this one. There was not a lot of light.

VISITORS WELCOME

As she grew, Debby realized she wanted to learn more about solar power. Solar power is electricity that comes from the sun. Solar panels are put on the roof of a building. The sunlight hits these panels and turns the sunlight into electricity.

Debby thought a lot about solar power. Then she had an **idea**! She was excited. She went to work for a company that provided solar power to people's homes. She believed it would be a good **solution** for people who had no electricity. Debby likes solving problems!

Solar Panels are now used on many homes.

Debby also thought of people in **villages** like the one she lived in as a child. The people in these small towns did not have any electricity. Solar power would work well there because there is a lot of sun in Arizona. Debby decided to help these families get solar power.

To get a family started, Debby helps them **borrow** money from a bank to buy the panels. After they get the money from the bank, they have some time to pay the money back. And the good news is there is no cost for using the sun's power!

Debby travels **across** lands outside cities in Arizona and New Mexico. She travels to the **countryside**. She helps Hopi and Navajo people get solar power.

Debby believes deeply in her work and **insists** that families learn about how solar power can help them. They are happy to do what she demands. Debby also travels to schools and summer camps to teach Hopi children about solar energy.

Debby helps many Hopi people.

Debby drives her truck from place to place. It is **lonely** with no one riding along. Then she thinks about how exciting it was to use electricity for the first time. Now families can do the things you do without thinking about them. They can heat their homes or turn on a light! Debby says she is, "lighting up people's lives."

Make Connections

How does Debby help her community? ESSENTIAL QUESTION

Talk with a partner about solar power. Could you use it where you live? TEXT TO SELF

Ask and Answer Questions

Asking yourself questions helps you think about information in the selection. You can ask questions before, during, and after you read.

Find Text Evidence

As I read page 216 of "Lighting Lives," I ask myself, "What is solar power?" I will reread to find the answer to this question.

page 216

As she grew, Debby realized she wanted to learn more about solar power. Solar power is electricity that comes from the sun. Solar panels are put on the roof of a building. The sunlight hits these panels and turns the sunlight into electricity.

Debby thought a lot about solar power. Then she had an idea. She was excited. She went

I read that solar power is electricity that comes from the sun. From this, I understand that solar panels use energy from the sun.

COLLABORATE

Your Turn

Think of a question about the selection. Reread the parts of the selection that help you answer the question.

Debby Tewa

Author's Purpose

Authors write to answer, explain, or describe.

 Find Text Evidence

When I read page 216 of "Lighting Lives," I learned how Debby Tewa got the idea to help others. I think this is a clue to the Author's Purpose.

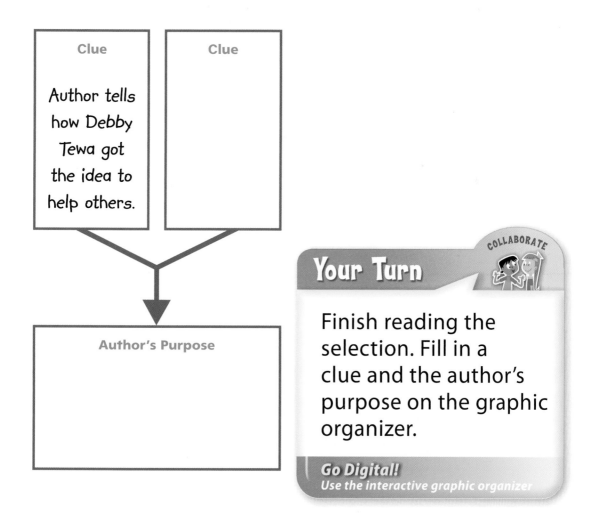

Clue	Clue
Author tells how Debby Tewa got the idea to help others.	

Author's Purpose

Your Turn

COLLABORATE

Finish reading the selection. Fill in a clue and the author's purpose on the graphic organizer.

Go Digital!
Use the interactive graphic organizer

Narrative Nonfiction

"Lighting Lives" is a narrative nonfiction.
A **narrative nonfiction:**
- tells a story about a person by a narrator.
- can have text features.

Find Text Evidence

I can use what I read to tell that "Lighting Lives," is narrative nonfiction. A narrator tells about a real person, Debby Tewa.

page 218

Debby travels **across** lands outside cities in Arizona and New Mexico. She travels to the **countryside**. She helps Hopi and Navajo people get solar power.

Debby believes deeply in her work and **insists** that families learn about how solar power can help them. They are happy to do what she demands. Debby also travels to schools and summer camps to teach Hopi children about solar energy.

Debby helps many Hopi people.

218

Text Features

Photos show something in the text or give more information about a topic.

Captions give information about the photo.

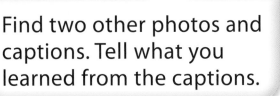

COLLABORATE

Your Turn

Find two other photos and captions. Tell what you learned from the captions.

Synonyms

Synonyms are words that have almost the same meaning. *Big* and *large* are synonyms.

 Find Text Evidence

I read that Debby "insists that families learn about how solar power can help them" and "They are happy to do what she demands." Insists and demands are synonyms. They both mean "asks for something in a strong or firm way."

> Debby believes deeply in her work and insists that families learn about how solar power can help them. They are happy to do what she demands.

Your Turn

 COLLABORATE

Think of a synonym for these words in "Lighting Lives."

home, *page 215*

power, *page 216*

Readers to...

The author of a selection uses voice to tell how someone in the writing feels about something. Reread the passage from "Lighting Lives."

Expert Model

Voice

What **opinion**, or feeling, words does the author use to show that solar power is important to Debby Tewa?

Debby thought a lot about solar power. Then she had an idea! She was excited. She went to work for a company that provided solar power to people's homes. She believed it would be a good solution for people who had no electricity. Debby likes solving problems!

Writers

Edwin wrote a narrative nonfiction selection. Read Edwin's writing.

Editing Marks

∧ Add.

ℛ Take out.

⊙ Add a period.

Grammar Handbook

Past Tense Verbs
See page 458.

Playing in the Snow

I live in hot, dry Arizona. Last winter, my family ~~drive~~ drove ∧ to Colorado. It was cold and snowing! Outside, I wore snow pants, a heavy coat, and snow boots ⊙ I loved the snow! I played outside for hours and hours. It was the best trip ~~trip~~ ever!

Your Turn

COLLABORATE

☑ Identify the opinion words Edwin used.
☑ Identify the past tense verbs.
☑ Tell how revisions improved his writing.

Go Digital!
Write online in Writer's Workspace

Essential Question

How does weather affect us?

Go Digital!

Nacivet/Photographer's Choice/Getty Images

226

Weather Affects Us

How do you prepare to go out in the event of rain? Do you wear a raincoat or carry an umbrella? Weather affects us in many ways.

▶ We dress differently for different kinds of weather.

▶ We go outside or stay indoors, depending on the weather.

Talk About It

Talk with a partner about the different kinds of weather. Then write each type of weather on the word web.

Vocabulary

Use the picture and sentence to learn each word.

damage

The storm caused some **damage** to the tree.

What kinds of damage can happen to a house?

dangerous

It is **dangerous** to ride a bike without a helmet.

What is the opposite of dangerous?

destroy

The puppy can **destroy** shoes by chewing on them.

What is the opposite of destroy?

event

The party was a fun **event** with food and games.

Tell about another event you have been to.

harsh The desert is a **harsh** place to live.

Name another harsh place to live.

prevent You should wash your hands to **prevent** sickness.

Tell how you can prevent yourself from being late to school.

warning Dark clouds are a **warning** that a storm is coming.

Tell about another warning that a storm is coming.

weather The **weather** is cold and snowy today.

Tell what the weather is like outside right now.

Your Turn

COLLABORATE

Pick three words. Write three questions for your partner to answer.

Go Digital! **Use the online visual glossary**

Tornado!

? Essential Question

How does weather affect us?

Read about how tornadoes form and how weather affects our lives.

What Is a Tornado?

The sky is dark far away. Something moves down from the clouds. It spins across the land. It sounds like a very loud train. A **tornado** is coming!

A tornado is a spinning cloud. It is shaped like a funnel. Its winds can reach 300 miles per hour. That is faster than a race car. The spinning air pulls things up. It can toss a car in the air. It can even **destroy**, or ruin a house. A tornado can be **dangerous**. It can cause harm to people and places.

When a funnel cloud reaches the ground, it becomes a tornado.

How Does a Tornado Form?

A tornado is a kind of **weather**. Weather is the condition of the air. Most tornadoes begin as a kind of weather called a **thunderstorm**. Thunderstorms are **harsh** rainstorms with thunder and lightning. These rough storms have high winds and heavy rain. When high winds spin and touch the ground, a tornado is born.

Most tornadoes do not stay on the ground for long. When they do, they can cause a lot of **damage**, or harm. A tornado is a big **event**!

Where Do Most Tornadoes Happen?

More tornadoes happen in the United States than anywhere in the world. Most of them form in the middle part of our country. Scientists think this might be because warm, wet air from the Gulf of Mexico crashes with the cool, dry air from Canada. This area is known as Tornado Alley.

Tornadoes can destroy trees, houses, and property.

How do Tornadoes Affect People?

Tornadoes affect people and towns in many ways. Weak tornadoes break branches from trees or damage signs. Strong tornadoes can destroy buildings.

People who live in areas where there are many tornadoes always think about the weather. They listen to the radio and watch news reports on television. Schools provide tornado drills so children can practice being safe in the event of a tornado. Teams of people work together to repair the damage caused by a tornado.

How Can You Stay Safe?

There are ways to **prevent**, or stop harm during a tornado. News reports use the words tornado **warning** to give notice that a tornado has been seen. Following safety rules can help everyone stay safe during a tornado!

People work together to clean up after a tornado.

Ways to  Stay Safe

1. Listen to weather reports.
2. Find shelter in a basement or room without windows.
3. Stay away from windows.
4. Listen to directions from a parent or teacher.

Make Connections

How do tornadoes affect us?
ESSENTIAL QUESTION

Compare what you read about tornadoes to an experience you have had with the weather. TEXT TO SELF

Ask and Answer Questions

When you read, asking questions helps you think about parts of the story and understand key details in the selection.

Find Text Evidence

As I read page 232 of "Tornado!" I ask myself, "What is a thunderstorm?" I will look for the answer to this question.

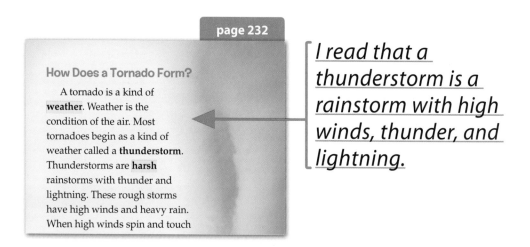

page 232

How Does a Tornado Form?

A tornado is a kind of **weather**. Weather is the condition of the air. Most tornadoes begin as a kind of weather called a **thunderstorm**. Thunderstorms are **harsh** rainstorms with thunder and lightning. These rough storms have high winds and heavy rain. When high winds spin and touch

I read that a thunderstorm is a rainstorm with high winds, thunder, and lightning.

COLLABORATE

Your Turn

As you reread page 234, think of a question. Continue rereading to find the answer to the question.

Main Idea and Key Details

The main idea is the most important point an author makes about a topic. Key details tell about and support the main idea.

 Find Text Evidence

As I read pages 231–232 of "Tornado!," I learned that tornadoes have powerful winds and can cause a lot of damage. These details support main idea of the text.

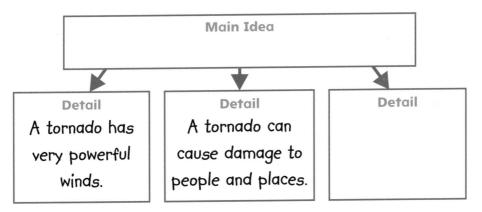

Main Idea

Detail	Detail	Detail
A tornado has very powerful winds.	A tornado can cause damage to people and places.	

COLLABORATE

Your Turn

Continue reading and fill in another key detail and the main idea on the graphic organizer.

Go Digital!
Use the interactive graphic organizer

Expository Text

"Tornado!" is an expository text.

Expository text:
- gives information about a topic.
- includes text features.

Find Text Evidence

I know "Tornado!" is an expository text because it gives information about tornadoes. It also has text features.

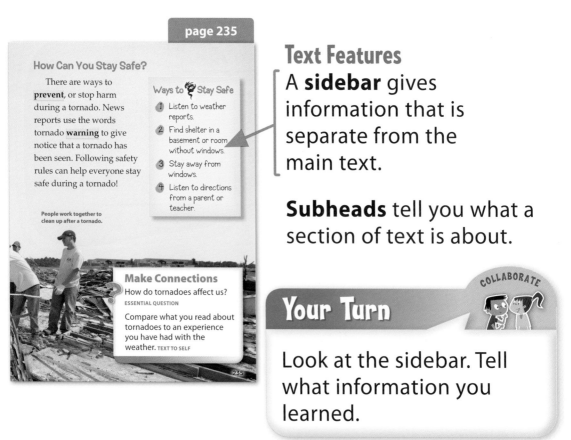

page 235

How Can You Stay Safe?

There are ways to **prevent**, or stop harm during a tornado. News reports use the words tornado **warning** to give notice that a tornado has been seen. Following safety rules can help everyone stay safe during a tornado!

People work together to clean up after a tornado.

Ways to 🌀 Stay Safe

1. Listen to weather reports.
2. Find shelter in a basement or room without windows.
3. Stay away from windows.
4. Listen to directions from a parent or teacher.

Make Connections

How do tornadoes affect us? ESSENTIAL QUESTION

Compare what you read about tornadoes to an experience you have had with the weather. TEXT TO SELF

235

Text Features

A **sidebar** gives information that is separate from the main text.

Subheads tell you what a section of text is about.

Your Turn

COLLABORATE

Look at the sidebar. Tell what information you learned.

Antonyms

Antonyms are two words that have opposite meanings. Words such as *hot* and *cold* are antonyms.

 Find Text Evidence

I see the author used the antonyms wet *and* dry *to show how wet air and dry air come together to make a tornado.*

> Scientists think this might be because warm, wet air from the Gulf of Mexico crashes with the cool, dry air from Canada.

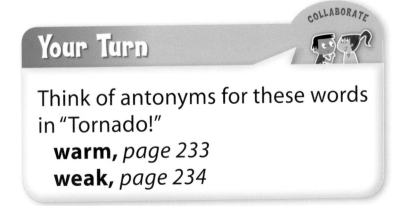

COLLABORATE

Your Turn

Think of antonyms for these words in "Tornado!"

warm, *page 233*

weak, *page 234*

Readers to...

Writers often organize nonfiction writing by giving a strong ending. Reread the passage from "Tornado!"

Organization
Identify a **strong ending** in the text. How does this help **organize** the writing?

How Can You Stay Safe?

There are ways to prevent, or stop, harm during a tornado. News reports use the words tornado warning to give notice that a tornado has been seen. Following safety rules can help keep everyone safe during a tornado!

Writers

Kim wrote an expository text. Read Kim's writing.

Editing Marks

∧ Add

ℊ Take out.

⊙ Add a period.

Grammar Handbook

Verb Have See page 484.

Student Model

Snowstorms

have

Snowstorms had lots of snow

and wind. The wind blows the

⊙

snow The snow piles up. If there

is a lot of snow, sometimes

play

schools are closed. Kids walk

in the snow. They build snowmen

sledding

and go riding. They also

have snowball fights.

Kids love snow!

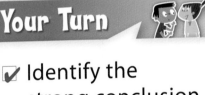

Your Turn

☑ Identify the strong conclusion Kim used.

☑ Identify her correction to the verb *had*.

☑ Tell how revisions improved her writing.

Go Digital!
Write online in Writer's Workspace

241

? Essential Question

How do you express yourself?

Go Digital!

Let's Communicate

People express themselves in many ways to show their feelings and share their thoughts. These boys are making music to express themselves. What are some ways you can express yourself?

▶ You can write, draw or paint.

▶ You can make music and sounds by playing an instrument or singing.

Talk About It COLLABORATE

Talk with a partner about ways you like to express yourselves. Then write your ideas on the web.

We Express Ourselves

Vocabulary

Use the picture and sentence to learn each word.

cheered We all **cheered** when our team won the game.

When would you cheer for something?

concert Jack and Luis played in the **concert** last night.

Tell about a concert that you have seen.

instrument A violin is a musical **instrument**.

Can you name another musical instrument?

movements The dancer's **movements** were graceful.

Describe the movements you make when you dance.

music Kira played her favorite kind of **music**.

What is your favorite kind of music?

rhythm They tapped the **rhythm** of the song.

What is another word for rhythm?

sounds The triangle and drum make different **sounds**.

What kind of sounds does a drum make if you hit it gently?

understand Ken did not **understand** the homework.

What should you do when you do not understand an assignment?

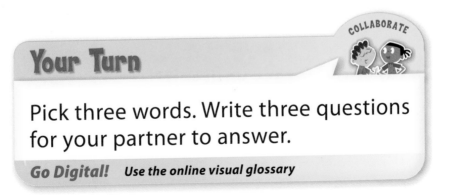

Your Turn

COLLABORATE

Pick three words. Write three questions for your partner to answer.

Go Digital! **Use the online visual glossary**

Essential Question

How do you express yourself?

Read about how children in a school chorus express themselves.

They've Got the Beat!

Some students in New York really sing their hearts out! That's because they are in the school chorus at Public School 22.

These students from Staten Island had a **concert** at the White House. They sang at a Hollywood awards show. Audiences have clapped and **cheered** them on. These kids are always asked to return.

How does it feel to sing on stage? "I get nervous singing for a big audience," Brianna Crispino recalls. "But when I see the joy on their faces, I get excited."

Brianna Crispino,
Public School 22 chorus member

Sounds Good

The P.S.22 chorus is divided into two groups. The sopranos sing high notes. The altos sing lower **sounds**. **Instruments** like drums sometimes keep the beat. It's important to keep the **rhythm** so they make the right sounds together.

Most adult choruses have four groups of voices. Here's a look at the number of each type of voice in one adult chorus from Pennsylvania.

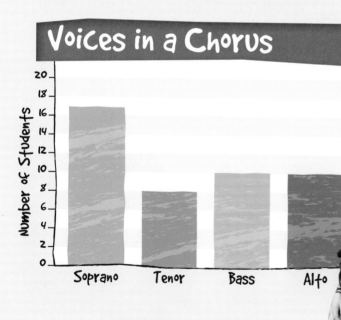

Voices in a Chorus

Gregg Breinberg, Public School 22 chorus teacher, plays piano to accompany the chorus.

Musical Expression

Being part of the chorus is hard work. The chorus members won't disagree. They practice for three hours each week.

Gregg Breinberg, their teacher, encourages the chorus to use **movements**. They move their hands to show how the songs make them feel. "They have their own movements because nobody feels **music** the same way," he explains.

The chorus members **understand** that singing in a chorus is a big job. "We just want to give it our best!" one student says.

Make Connections

How do the singers in the chorus express themselves?
ESSENTIAL QUESTION

How is this the same or different from what you know about singing? **TEXT TO SELF**

Bebeto Matthews/AP Images

Ask and Answer Questions

When you read, asking questions helps you think about key details of the text that you may have missed or do not understand.

Find Text Evidence

As I read page 247 of "They've Got the Beat!" I ask myself, "What is it like for the students to sing at the White House?" I will reread to find the answer.

page 247

at a Hollywood awards show. Audiences have clapped and **cheered** them on. These kids are always asked to return.

How does it feel to sing on stage? "I get nervous singing for a big audience," Brianna Crispino recalls. "But when I see the joy on their faces, I get excited."

Brianna Crispino, Public School 22 chorus member

247

I reread that a chorus member says that she gets nervous at first. Then it becomes exciting.

Your Turn

COLLABORATE

Think of a question you have about the selection. Reread the parts of the story that help you answer the question.

Main Idea and Key Details

The main idea is the most important point an author makes about a topic. Key details tell about and support the main idea.

 Find Text Evidence

As I read page 247 of "They've Got the Beat," I understand a key detail about this chorus is that they have performed at famous places.

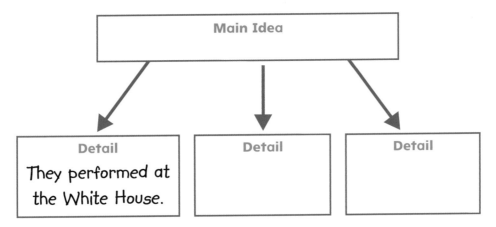

Main Idea

Detail	Detail	Detail
They performed at the White House.		

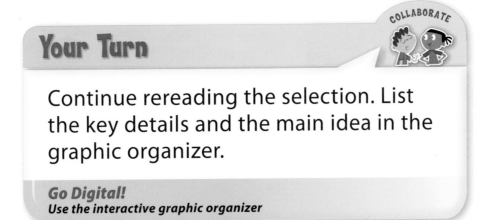

Your Turn

Continue rereading the selection. List the key details and the main idea in the graphic organizer.

Go Digital!
Use the interactive graphic organizer

Expository Text

"They've Got the Beat!" is an expository text.
Expository text:
- gives facts and information about a topic.
- can have a graph, photos and captions.

Find Text Evidence

I know "They've Got the Beat!" is an expository text. It gives information about real students. It has a graph with facts about a chorus.

page 248

Sounds Good

The P.S.22 chorus is divided into two groups. The sopranos sing high notes. The altos sing lower **sounds**. **Instruments** like drums sometimes keep the beat. It's important to keep the **rhythm** so they make the right sounds together.

Most adult choruses have four groups of voices. Here's a look at the number of each type of voice in one adult chorus from Pennsylvania.

Voices in a Chorus

Number of Students
20, 18, 16, 14, 12, 10, 8, 6, 4, 2, 0

Soprano Tenor Bass Alto

Gregg Breinberg, Public School 22 Chorus teacher, plays piano to accompany the chorus.

248

Text Features

A **bar graph** uses bars to give information about a topic.

COLLABORATE

Your Turn

Tell what information you learned from looking at the bar graph.

Prefixes

A prefix is a word part at the beginning of a word. You can separate the root word from a prefix, such as *re-* or *ex-* to figure out the meaning of the word.

 Find Text Evidence

I'm not sure what the word "return" means. I know the word turn *means to move around in a circle. The prefix* re- *means* again. *The word* return *means to come around again.*

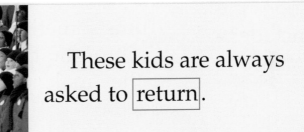

These kids are always asked to return .

Your Turn

COLLABORATE

Use the prefixes to figure out the meanings of these words in "They've Got the Beat!"

recalls, *page 247*

disagree, *page 249*

Carrie Devorah/WENN.com/Newscom

Readers to...

Writers use long and short sentences to add interest to their writing. Reread the passage from "They've Got the Beat!"

Sentence Fluency

What examples of short and long **sentence length** does the writer include?

The P.S.22 chorus is divided into two groups. The sopranos sing high notes. The altos sing lower sounds. Instruments like drums sometimes keep the beat. It's important to keep the rhythm so they make the right sounds together.

Most adult chorus have four groups of voices. Here's a look at the number of each type of voice in one adult chorus from Pennsylvania.

Bebeto Matthews/AP Images

Writers

Editing Marks

∧ Add

ⸯ Take out.

/ Make a small letter.

Grammar Handbook

Combining Sentences
See page 476.

Nikki wrote a newspaper review about her favorite song. Read Nikki's revision.

Student Model

Tomorrow Is Here

The new singing group Tunes came out with a great new song called "Tomorrow Is Here." The song has a catchy beat. You
                                    and
cannot help but tap your feet. ~~Why not listen to it today?~~ The words are easy to sing, too.

Why not listen to it today?
∧

Your Turn

COLLABORATE

☑ Identify the sentence lengths Nikki used.

☑ Find two sentences Nikki combined or moved.

☑ Tell how revisions improved her writing.

Go Digital!
Write online in Writer's Workspace

Unit 4

Our Life, Our World

The Big idea

Oh! What a World!

Oh, what a world!
What a wonderful place,
Spinning round and round in space.

Desert winds blow to and fro,
Deep, wide rivers ripple, flow,
Mountaintops wear caps of snow,
Lush, green jungles grow and GROW.

Oh, what a world!
What a wonderful place,
Spinning round and round in space.

— **by George Samos**

Corinna Ice

Essential Question

What makes different parts of the world different?

Go Digital!

New Places

Have you ever been to a forest? This region offers tall trees and many plants and animals. There are many different regions around the world. Here are a few:

▶ Deserts

▶ Polar Regions

▶ Prairies

Talk About It

What is it like where you live? Talk to a partner about your location. Write your ideas on the web.

Our Region

Vocabulary

Use the picture and sentence to learn each word.

eerie The noises in the old barn gave me an **eerie** feeling.

When do you get an eerie feeling?

growth I found a thick **growth** of ferns in the park.

During what season do you see a new growth of plants?

layers It was cold so I wore three **layers** of clothing.

How many layers of clothing are you wearing today?

lively The **lively** kitten played with a ball.

What activity makes you feel lively?

location

I can find the **location** of my state on a map.

What is another word for location?

region

The arctic **region** is very cold and snowy.

What region is very hot and dry?

seasons

Summer is our favorite of all the **seasons**.

Describe your favorite season.

temperate

A **temperate** climate is not too hot or too cold.

Explain whether a desert would have a temperate climate.

COLLABORATE

Your Turn

Pick three words. Write three questions for your partner to answer.

Go Digital! **Use the online visual glossary**

Alaska

A Special Place

? Essential Question

What makes different parts of the world different?

Read to learn what makes Alaska unique.

Where can you find mountains, glaciers, and volcanoes? Alaska is the **location** you would visit. Alaska has different **regions**. In each part of the state, there are different features.

Land Features

The tallest mountain in the United States is in Alaska. It is called Mt. McKinley. Some people go to Alaska just to climb it.

Alaska also has the biggest glaciers in all of the United States. Glaciers are made when one **layer** of snow falls on top of another. The snowfall becomes very thick. It turns to ice. The **growth** of a glacier takes many years to form.

Map of Alaska

Alaska

Juneau

Key
★ Capital
≈ Rivers
⌒ Mountains
▲ Volcanoes

TSJ Graphics

Temperature Changes

Alaska has different temperatures. Northern Alaska is called the Arctic region. The temperatures are much colder than inside your freezer. The ground, lakes, and rivers are almost always frozen.

As a result, most people live in the south of Alaska. It is warmer there. Crops grow well in the rich soil there.

Animals

Alaska has many different animals. You may spot a walrus or polar bear among the glaciers. You can see a black or brown bear fishing in a river or stream. In another region, you can see a moose or caribou.

Walruses live in shallow waters off the coast of Alaska.

Daylight and Darkness

The **seasons** are special here, too. In summer, people celebrate the mild **temperate** weather. These **lively** people also celebrate the sunlight because the sun does not set for many days. In one village, the Sun doesn't set for more than 80 days! You might be in bed and still see the sun shining.

In winter, the Sun doesn't rise in some places in Alaska. These places have more than 60 days of winter darkness. You could have afternoon soccer practice in the dark! You might think this would be **eerie,** but Alaskans don't think this is weird. They are used to the dark winter days.

Alaska is a very interesting place to live!

Make Connections

What are three things that make Alaska interesting? ESSENTIAL QUESTION

How is where you live different from Alaska? How is it the same? TEXT TO SELF

Reread

As you read, you may come across words, facts, or explanations that are new to you. You can reread these parts to make sure you understand them.

 Find Text Evidence

After reading page 263 of "Alaska: A Special Place," I am not sure how glaciers form. I will reread this page.

page 263

Land Features

The tallest mountain in the United States is in Alaska. It is called Mt. McKinley. Some people go to Alaska just to climb it.

Alaska also has the biggest glaciers in all of the United States. Glaciers are made when one **layer** of snow falls on top of another. The snowfall becomes very thick. It turns to ice. The **growth** of a glacier takes many years to form.

I read that over time, layers of snow turn to ice. These huge pieces of ice are glaciers. Rereading helped me understand this part.

Your Turn

What is the Arctic region? Reread page 264 of "Alaska: A Special Place" to answer the question.

Compare and Contrast

To compare is to tell how things are alike.
To contrast is to tell how they are different.

Find Text Evidence

*When I read page 263 of "Alaska: A Special Place,"
I can compare and contrast the land features in
Alaska.*

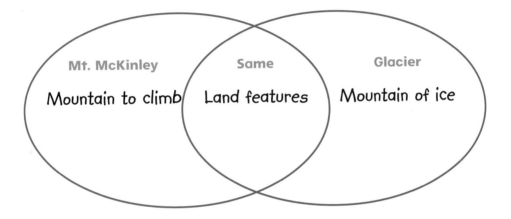

Mt. McKinley

Same

Glacier

Mountain to climb

Land features

Mountain of ice

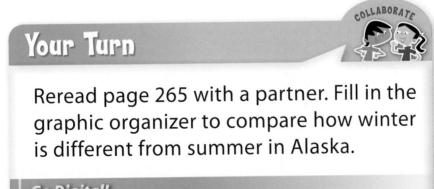

Your Turn

COLLABORATE

Reread page 265 with a partner. Fill in the
graphic organizer to compare how winter
is different from summer in Alaska.

Go Digital!
Use the interactive graphic organizer

Expository Text

"Alaska: A Special Place" is an expository text.

Expository text:
- gives facts and information about a topic.
- includes text features.

 Find Text Evidence

"Alaska: A Special Place" is an expository text. It gives facts about Alaska. We also learn about Alaska by looking at the text features.

page 263

Where can you find mountains, glaciers, and volcanoes? Alaska is the **location** you would visit. Alaska has different **regions**. In each part of the state, there are different features.

Land Features

The tallest mountain in the United States is in Alaska. It is called Mt. McKinley. Some people go to Alaska just to climb it.

Alaska also has the biggest glaciers in all of the United States. Glaciers are made when one **layer** of snow falls on top of another. The snowfall becomes very thick. It turns to ice. The **growth** of a glacier takes many years to form.

Map of Alaska

Alaska

Key
★ Capital
≈ Rivers
▲ Mountains
▲ Volcanoes

Juneau

263

Text Features

A **map** is a flat picture of part of the earth.

A **map key** tells you what symbols on a map mean.

Your Turn

COLLABORATE

Talk about what information you learned from the map and map key.

Compound Words

A compound word is made up of two smaller words. You can put together the meanings of each smaller word to help you learn the meaning of the compound word.

 Find Text Evidence

In the word snowfall, *I see two smaller words:* snow *and* fall. *I think* snowfall *means snow that falls to the ground. Yes, that makes sense in this sentence.*

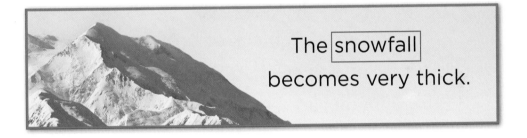

The snowfall
becomes very thick.

COLLABORATE

Your Turn

Use the smaller words to figure out the meanings of these compound words in "Alaska: A Special Place."

sunlight, *page 265*

afternoon, *page 265*

John R. Delapp/Photolibrary

269

Readers to...

In expository text, writers choose a topic to write about. They include facts that tell about the topic. Reread the passage from "Alaska: A Special Place."

Ideas
What **topic** does the writer give facts about?

Expert Model

Animals

Alaska has many different animals. You may spot a walrus or polar bear among the glaciers. You can see a black or brown bear fishing in a river or stream. In another region, you can see a moose or caribou.

Steven J. Kazlowski/Alamy

Writers

Julia wrote an expository text.
Read Julia's writing.

Editing Marks

≡ Make a capital letter.

∧ Add

✗ Take out.

Grammar Handbook
Linking Verbs
See page 481.

Student Model

Alaska

Alaska ^is^ very different from

where I live! In the summer

where I live, it is hot. ≡the sun

sets after dinner. In parts of

Alaska, the sun does not go

down in summer! Where I

live, it doesn't snow. In Alaska

it snows a lot in

the ~~summer~~ ^winter^.

Your Turn   COLLABORATE

- ☑ Identify Julia's topic.
- ☑ Identify a linking verb.
- ☑ Tell how revisions improved her writing.

Go Digital!
Write online in Writer's Workspace

? **Essential Question**

How does the Earth change?

Go Digital!

Michael Melford/Riser/Getty Images

Our Changing Earth

Did you know that the Earth is always changing? The water in this canyon is slowly washing away the rocks. Water can have powerful properties.

▶ Water can wash away rocks and land in rivers and waterfalls.

▶ Water can wash away sand at the beach.

Talk About It

COLLABORATE

Talk with a partner about what could cause the Earth to change quickly. Write your ideas on the web.

Earth Changes

Vocabulary

Use the picture and sentence to learn each word.

active

The **active** volcano was about to erupt.

What do you like to do when you want to be active?

earth

We dug into the **earth** to plant some lettuce.

What else can you plant in the earth?

explode

Fireworks make bright colors and loud noises as they **explode**.

Name something else that can explode.

island

We visited an **island** on our vacation.

What are some things you can find on an island?

(t) Corbis; (tc) Patrick Lane/Somos RF/Getty Images; (bc) Ron Chapple/Comstock Images/Getty Images; (b) Image Ideas/PictureQuest

local Grandpa and I went to a **local** park.

Tell about some places that are local to your house.

properties I looked at the rock to learn about its **properties**.

Tell about some properties of a pencil.

solid Wood is **solid**, but water and air are not.

How can you tell if something is solid?

steep This hill is **steep** and hard to climb.

What else can be steep?

Your Turn

COLLABORATE

Pick three words. Write three questions for your partner to answer.

Go Digital! **Use the online visual glossary**

Into the Sea

Essential Question

How does the Earth change?

Read to learn how ocean waves change beaches over time.

What Is Erosion?

Have you ever made a sand castle at the beach? You must pick a good spot for it. If it is too close to the water, waves will quickly wash it away.

Ocean waves and wind can also wash away land. They can change the shape of an **island**, which is land circled by water. When wind and water change the shape of **Earth**, it is called **erosion**.

Waves are the biggest cause of erosion at the beach. Ocean waves are always **active** and moving onto the shore. They carry the sand away bit by bit.

Strong waves are one of the **properties** of big storms. These waves **explode** as they crash onto the beach. Storm waves can move a lot of sand quickly.

Before Erosion

After Erosion

Erosion of Beaches

Some people build houses near the ocean. Waves take away the sand between the houses and the sea. As the beach disappears, the water gets closer to houses and other **solid** buildings on the beach. Some buildings can even be washed away.

Erosion of Rocks

Erosion also happens on **steep**, rocky cliffs or sharp slopes. First, waves smash into the bottom of the cliffs. Then they carry away tiny pieces of rock. Over time, many small pieces of rock wash away from the bottom of the cliff. This makes the top of the cliff weak. The cliff can crumble and fall into the sea.

Stopping Erosion

Some **local** communities work to stop erosion to nearby beaches. These towns have built **sea walls** of large boulders or rocks.

The rocks are placed in a row in the sea. When waves hit the sea wall, they slow down. Then the waves can't pull sand away.

Some towns make rules about buildings on the beach. New buildings must be far from the water. Then they won't wash away like a sand castle.

Make Connections

? How does beach erosion change the Earth? ESSENTIAL QUESTION

How do the changes from erosion in this selection compare to other changes in nature you have seen? TEXT TO SELF

Presselect/Alamy

Reread

As you read, you may come across words, facts, or explanations that you do not understand. Rereading can help you understand them.

Find Text Evidence

As I read page 277 of "Into the Sea," I am not sure I understand erosion. I will reread this section.

---

page 277

Ocean waves and wind can also wash away land. They can change the shape of an **island**, which is land circled by water. When wind and water change the shape of **Earth**, it is called **erosion**.

Waves are the biggest cause of erosion at the beach. Ocean waves are always **active** and moving onto the shore. They carry the sand away bit by bit.

Strong waves are one of the **properties**

I read that erosion is when waves and wind change the shape of the earth. Rereading helped me understand what erosion is.

COLLABORATE

Your Turn

Why is erosion a problem? Reread page 278 of "Into the Sea" to answer the question.

Cause and Effect

A cause is an event or action that makes something happen. An effect is what happens because of that event.

 Find Text Evidence

On page 277 of "Into the Sea" I read that erosion can take sand away from the beach. This is the cause. I ask "What happens when the sand gets washed away?" This will help me understand the effect.

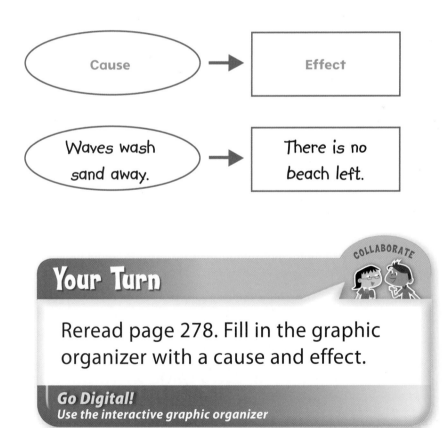

| Cause | → | Effect |

| Waves wash sand away. | → | There is no beach left. |

COLLABORATE

Your Turn

Reread page 278. Fill in the graphic organizer with a cause and effect.

Go Digital!
Use the interactive graphic organizer

Expository Text

The selection "Into the Sea" is an expository text.

Expository text:
- includes facts about real events.
- includes text features.
- has a text structure.

🔍 Find Text Evidence

"Into the Sea" is an expository text. I can tell it is expository because it has causes and effects about real events. It also has text features.

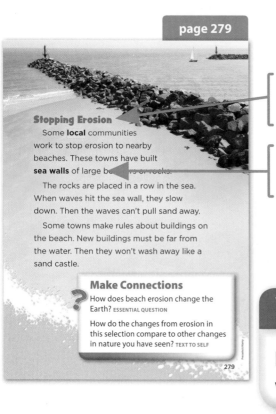

page 279

Stopping Erosion

Some **local** communities work to stop erosion to nearby beaches. These towns have built **sea walls** of large bo...ks or rocks.

The rocks are placed in a row in the sea. When waves hit the sea wall, they slow down. Then the waves can't pull sand away.

Some towns make rules about buildings on the beach. New buildings must be far from the water. Then they won't wash away like a sand castle.

Make Connections

? How does beach erosion change the Earth? ESSENTIAL QUESTION

How do the changes from erosion in this selection compare to other changes in nature you have seen? TEXT TO SELF

279

Text Features

A **subhead** tells what the section of text is about.

Bold print is important to understanding the selection.

COLLABORATE

Your Turn

Reread page 279. Talk about why sea walls are important.

Context Clues

As you read, you can figure out a word you do not know by looking at the words and sentences near it for clues to its meaning.

Find Text Evidence

I'm not sure what the word communities *means. To figure out what it means, I read on, looking for clues. I see the word* towns *used in the next sentence. I think* communities *means "towns."*

> Some local communities work to stop erosion to nearby beaches. These towns have built sea walls of large boulders or rocks.

Your Turn

COLLABORATE

Use clues in the sentences to figure out the meanings of these words in "Into the Sea."
crumble, *page 278*
boulders, *page 279*

Presselect/Alamy

Readers to...

Writers sometimes use time-order words to help you understand the order of events. Reread the passage from "Into the Sea."

Word Choice
What **time order words** does the writer use to explain how erosion happens?

Paul Thompson Images/Alamy

Expert Model

Erosion also happens on steep, rocky cliffs or sharp slopes. First, waves smash into the bottom of the cliffs. Then they carry away tiny pieces of rock. Over time, many small pieces of rock wash away from the bottom of the cliff. This makes the top of the cliff weak. The cliff can crumble and fall into the sea.

Writers

Meg wrote an expository text. Read Meg's revision.

Editing Marks

/ Make a small letter.

⊙ Add a period.

∧ Add

⌐ Take out.

Grammar Handbook

Helping Verbs
See pages 485.

Student Model

Erosion

First,
∧Waves wash away sand from

beaches. This is called erosion.

This causes the beach to wash

~~wash~~ away over time. Then

⊙
/There is not much beach left∧

After the sand is gone, people

will not go to the beach.

Your Turn

COLLABORATE

☑ Identify the time-order words Meg used.

☑ Identify the helping verbs.

☑ Tell how revisions improved her writing.

Go Digital!
Write online in Writer's Workspace

Essential Question

How are kids around the world different?

Go Digital!

Floresco Productions/Corbis

Around the World

This is a game called cricket. It is a common game in many countries around the world. The game is played with two teams.

▶ You use a bat and a ball.

▶ You hit the ball and run towards the other end of the field to score.

Talk About It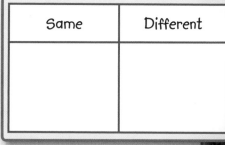

Think of some games that are special to your culture. Talk with a partner and tell how they are the same or different from cricket. Write your ideas on the chart.

Same	Different

Vocabulary

Use the picture and sentence to learn each word.

common

Tag is a **common** game that children like.

What are some common places to go in your neighborhood?

costume

Each actor in the play wore a colorful **costume**.

When else might people wear costumes?

customs

A turkey dinner and a family gathering are Thanksgiving **customs**.

Tell about your holiday customs.

favorite

Autumn is our **favorite** season, because we like cool weather best.

What is your favorite season?

parades

Our band marches in town **parades**.

What do you like about parades?

surrounded

We were **surrounded** by flowers.

How might you travel to a place surrounded by water?

travels

The car **travels** along the road.

What travels along a track?

wonder

I **wonder** when it will stop raining.

What are some things you wonder about?

COLLABORATE

Your Turn

Pick three words. Write three questions for your partner to answer.

Go Digital! *Use the online visual glossary*

Happy New Year!

? Essential Question

How are kids around the world different?

Read about a girl celebrating the New Year holiday in the United States and China.

Susan Swan

I celebrated the New Year twice in one year. Do you **wonder** how? I celebrated the holiday in the United States and then in China.

On December 31, our city had a celebration to welcome the New Year. This celebration began with a **parade**. A band played music, and I got my face painted like a lion. Then I watched a man carve animals from ice. We were **surrounded** by fun!

Just before midnight, everyone went to the park. The crowd counted down the last seconds of the old year. Then came my **favorite** part, the thing I like most. Pop! Pop! Pop! Fireworks like a shower of colorful lights sprinkled down from the sky.

Then my family took a plane to China. A plane is huge and **travels** over the ocean like a whale in the sky. We celebrated Chinese New Year with Grandma. This celebration is different than in the United States. It lasts for fifteen days, not just one night. After we arrived, Grandma surprised me with new red clothing. She said red brings good luck.

On New Year's Eve, we went to Grandma's house. I learned many interesting Chinese **customs**. One custom is to have a family dinner that includes tasty dumplings. Then we stepped outdoors to watch a big parade. At the end, a rainbow of firecrackers snapped and popped in the sky!

Susan Swan

Later that week we watched the Chinese lion dance. I'd never seen anything like it. Each pair of dancers wore a fancy lion **costume** made of cloth as yellow as the Sun. The dancers leaped through the air and did amazing tricks!

We went to the Lantern Festival on the last day of Chinese New Year. The full moon hung like a balloon in the dark sky. Everyone made paper lanterns that lit up the night.

The two celebrations were different. They were the same, too. They had one thing in **common**. They were both exciting family celebrations to welcome the New Year!

Make Connections

How is the New Year celebration in China different from the celebration in the United States? ESSENTIAL QUESTION

Compare the New Year's celebrations in the story to how you and your family celebrate the New Year. TEXT TO SELF

CCSS **Comprehension Strategy**

Visualize

When you visualize, you use the author's words to form pictures in your mind about a story.

Find Text Evidence

After reading page 291 of "Happy New Year," I used the author's words to help me visualize what was happening in the story.

> **page 291**
>
> On December 31, our city had a celebration to welcome the New Year. This celebration began with a **parade**. A band played music, and I got my face painted like a lion. Then I watched a man carve animals from ice. We were **surrounded** by fun!
>
> Just before midnight, everyone went to the park. The crowd counted down the last seconds of the old year. Then came my **favorite** part, the thing I like most. Pop! Pop! Pop! Fireworks like a shower of colorful lights sprinkled down from the sky.

I read that there was a band playing music and the girl got her face painted like a lion. This helps me visualize the story.

Your Turn

Reread page 293. What words help you visualize the Chinese lion dance?

Compare and Contrast

When you compare events in a story, you look for ways they are alike. When you contrast events, you tell how they are different.

 Find Text Evidence

On page 292 of "Happy New Year!" I can compare how long the Chinese New Year and the United States New Year last.

	United States Celebration	Chinese Celebration
How long it lasts	one night	fifteen days
Activities		

Your Turn

Continue rereading the story. Compare and contrast the information and fill information in the graphic organizer.

Go Digital!
Use the interactive graphic organizer

Realistic Fiction

The story "Happy New Year!" is realistic fiction.
Realistic fiction:

- has made-up characters, settings, and events that could be real.
- is sometimes written in the first person.

Find Text Evidence

I can tell that "Happy New Year!" is realistic fiction. The events in this story could be real events. The story is told by a person who could be real.

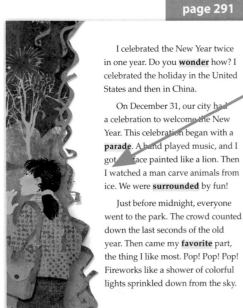

page 291

I celebrated the New Year twice in one year. Do you **wonder** how? I celebrated the holiday in the United States and then in China.

On December 31, our city had a celebration to welcome the New Year. This celebration began with a **parade**. A band played music, and I got my face painted like a lion. Then I watched a man carve animals from ice. We were **surrounded** by fun!

Just before midnight, everyone went to the park. The crowd counted down the last seconds of the old year. Then came my **favorite** part, the thing I like most. Pop! Pop! Pop! Fireworks like a shower of colorful lights sprinkled down from the sky.

291

Story Structure

Realistic fiction sometimes uses **first person**. A character uses words, such as *I, me, we, our, my,* or *us* to tell the story.

Your Turn

COLLABORATE

Give two more examples of how you know this story is realistic fiction.

Similes

A simile uses the words *like* or *as* to compare two different things. To understand a simile, figure out how an author compares one thing to another.

Find Text Evidence

I read a plane "travels over the ocean like a whale in the sky." I see the word like, *so the author must be using a simile. I think the author is comparing the large size of the plane to the size of a whale.*

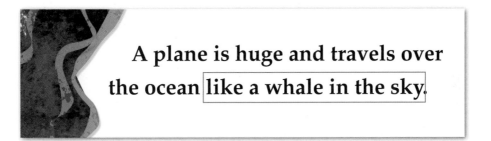

A plane is huge and travels over the ocean like a whale in the sky.

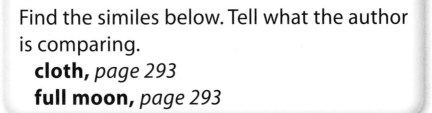

Your Turn

COLLABORATE

Find the similes below. Tell what the author is comparing.

cloth, *page 293*

full moon, *page 293*

Readers to...

Writers use voice to show their feelings. Writers may show their excitement or interest about a topic. Reread the passage from "Happy New Year!"

Expert Model

Voice
How does the speaker **show feelings** in this passage?

Later that week we watched the Chinese lion dance. I'd never seen anything like it. Each pair of dancers wore a fancy lion costume made of cloth as yellow as the Sun. The dancers leaped through the air and did amazing tricks!

Susan Swan

Writers

Jenny wrote a letter to her friend.
Read Jenny's letter.

Grammar Handbook
Irregular Verbs,
See page 486.

Student Model

Dear Bella,

How was your Fourth of
July? I had the *best* holiday!

Every year, our family goes to
the lake. The weather was really
hot, so we swam. Then we ^eated^ (ate)
dinner by the lake. Finally, it was
time for the fireworks⊙ I liked
the ^giant^ purple fireworks the best!

Your friend,

Jenny

Your Turn
COLLABORATE

- ☑ Identify the feelings Jenny shows in her letter.
- ☑ Identify an irregular verb.
- ☑ Tell how revisions improved her writing.

Go Digital!
Write online in Writer's Workspace

Essential Question

How can we understand nature?

Go Digital!

Stories About Nature

Have you ever seen a beetle with such bright colors? For years, people have been trying to explain nature through stories. Here are some questions people have tried to answer:

▶ Why does a zebra have stripes?

▶ Why is the sky blue?

Talk About It

COLLABORATE

Work with a partner. Think of some questions you have about nature. Write your questions on the web.

Nature Questions

Vocabulary

Use the picture and sentence to learn each word.

ashamed

Kim felt **ashamed** that she hurt her friend's feelings.

Describe how you feel when you are ashamed.

boast

They always **boast** that they are the best team.

What are some things people might boast about?

dash

People had to **dash** to get out of the rain.

How do you move when you dash somewhere?

holler

I heard Sandy **holler** for her dog.

When else might someone holler?

plenty

There was **plenty** of fresh corn at the picnic.

What is something you have plenty of?

similarities

There are many **similarities** between my brother and me.

What is the opposite of similarities?

victory

Winning the race was a great **victory** for our team.

Tell about a victory you have had.

wisdom

Grandpa used his **wisdom** to help me solve my problem.

Tell how you know someone has wisdom.

COLLABORATE

Your Turn

Pick three words. Write three questions for your partner to answer.

Go Digital! **Use the online visual glossary**

Why the Sun and Moon Live in the Sky

? Essential Question

How can we understand nature?

Read about how the sun and the moon ended up in the sky.

Mike Litwin

This play is based on an African folktale that tells how the moon and sun ended up in the sky.

Narrator: Long ago, Sun, Moon, and Water lived together on Earth.

(Sun and Moon are eating breakfast at home.)

Sun: I will visit my good friend Water today.

Moon: That sounds enjoyable, but why doesn't Water ever visit us? Do you feel **ashamed** or embarrassed to invite Water here?

Sun: No, I am proud of our house. I will invite Water today!

(Sun visits Water at the beach.)

Sun: Water, why don't you ever visit us?

Water: Your house can't hold me and my family.

Sun: That's nonsense! Moon and I will enlarge our house, so there will be **plenty** of room for everyone!

Water: Then I will visit you.

Sun: Wonderful! Please **holler** loudly, so I hear you when you arrive. Now I must **dash** home quickly to start the work.

(Sun rushes home.)

Narrator: Sun and Moon raced to make their home larger. They added rooms and raised the roof higher. The new house was completely different and had no **similarities** to their old home. They felt it was a **victory**, or a win, for now their friend could visit.

Water: Sun and Moon, I have arrived!

Mike Litwin

Sun: Isn't this the largest home you've seen?

Moon: Sun, it's not polite to brag, so please don't **boast** to our guest. Water, come inside.

Narrator: Water splashed through the door carrying colorful fish, frogs, and crabs. As the water began to rise, Sun and Moon climbed onto furniture. Then they scrambled onto the roof.

Sun: Moon, I'm not sure about the **wisdom** of inviting Water. Perhaps this wasn't a smart idea!

Moon: No, Sun, it was the right thing to do but we must fly to safety!

Narrator: Sun and Moon flew to the sky, where they remain today and still shine down on Water.

Make Connections

What does this folktale explain about nature? **ESSENTIAL QUESTION**

How is this story different from what you know about the sun and moon? **TEXT TO SELF**

Visualize

When you visualize, you form pictures in your mind about the character, setting, and plot of the story.

Find Text Evidence

As I read page 307 of "Why the Sun and Moon Live in the Sky," I can visualize what is happening in the story.

> **page 307**
>
> **Sun:** Isn't this the largest home you've seen?
>
> **Moon:** Sun, it's not polite to brag, so please don't **boast** to our guest. Water, come inside.
>
> **Narrator:** Water splashed through the door carrying colorful fish, frogs, and crabs. As the water began to rise, Sun and Moon climbed onto furniture. Then they scrambled onto the roof.
>
> **Sun:** Moon, I'm not sure about the **wisdom** of inviting Water. Perhaps this wasn't a smart idea!
>
> **Moon:** No, Sun, it was the right thing to do but we must fly to safety!
>
> **Narrator:** Sun and Moon flew to the sky, where they remain today and still shine down

I read that water splashed through the door carrying colorful fish, frogs and crabs. This helps me visualize what is happening in the story.

Your Turn

COLLABORATE

What was it like when Sun and Moon enlarged their house? Reread page 306 and tell what you visualize.

Mike Litwin

Theme

The theme of a story is the main message the author wants to tell the reader. To find the theme, think about what the characters say and do.

 Find Text Evidence

On page 306 of "Why the Sun and Moon Live in the Sky," Sun and Moon make their house bigger so water can visit. This is a clue that the theme is about friendship.

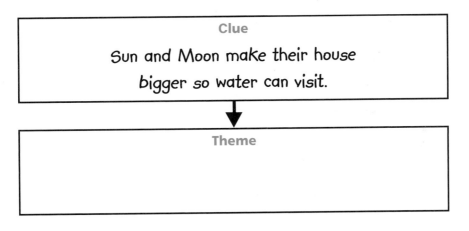

Clue
Sun and Moon make their house bigger so water can visit.

↓

Theme

COLLABORATE

Your Turn

Reread the play. Find another clue and then write the theme in the graphic organizer.

Go Digital!
Use the interactive graphic organizer

Drama

"Why the Sun and Moon Live in the Sky" is a drama that tells a folktale.

A drama:

- is a play that can be acted out on stage.
- has parts that characters speak aloud.
- can have a lesson to be learned

Find Text Evidence

I can tell that "Why the Sun and Moon Live in the Sky" is a drama. It is written with parts for the characters.

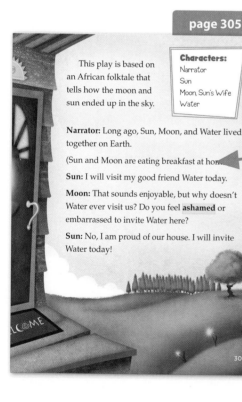

page 305

This play is based on an African folktale that tells how the moon and sun ended up in the sky.

Characters:
Narrator
Sun
Moon, Sun's Wife
Water

Narrator: Long ago, Sun, Moon, and Water lived together on Earth.

(Sun and Moon are eating breakfast at home.)

Sun: I will visit my good friend Water today.

Moon: That sounds enjoyable, but why doesn't Water ever visit us? Do you feel **ashamed** or embarrassed to invite Water here?

Sun: No, I am proud of our house. I will invite Water today!

305

Story Structure

I see that each character has **dialogue**. Dialogue is the words that each character says in a drama.

COLLABORATE

Your Turn

Reread the play with a partner. Then talk about the lesson learned from this drama of a folktale.

Root Words

To understand the meaning of a word you do not know, try to separate the root word from its ending or suffix, such as *-ed, -ly,* or *-able.*

 Find Text Evidence

I'm not sure what enjoyable *means so I separate the root word* enjoy *from the suffix* -able. *I know that* enjoy *means "like" and the suffix* -able *means 'able to.' I think* enjoyable *means "something you like to do."*

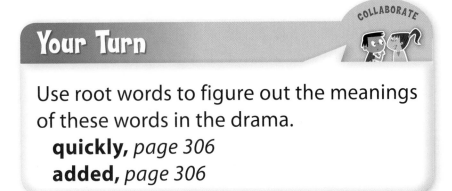

That sounds enjoyable, but why doesn't Water ever visit us?

Your Turn

COLLABORATE

Use root words to figure out the meanings of these words in the drama.

quickly, *page 306*

added, *page 306*

Readers to...

To develop a character, writers tell the character's experiences and thoughts. Reread the passage from "Why the Sun and Moon Live in the Sky."

Ideas

Tell how the writer **develops characters**. What can you tell about the characters from these details?

Expert Model

Sun: Moon, I'm not sure about the wisdom of inviting Water. Perhaps this wasn't a smart idea!

Moon: No, Sun, it was the right thing to do but we must fly to safety!

Writers

Frank wrote a new ending for the drama. Read Frank's ending.

Editing Marks

= Make a capital letter.

⊙ Add a period.

∧ Add.

⟋ Take out.

Grammar Handbook

Irregular Verbs, See page 486.

Student Model

Sun and Moon Move to the Sky

Moon: Water brought too many

friends. They ~~maked~~ made ∧ a big mess

in our new house! You must ask

them to leave⊙

Sun: I am sorry. ∧ I have a better idea. Let's

move to a new house. look up

in the sky! We can have a big

house there. Come,

Moon, let's go!

Your Turn   COLLABORATE

- ☑ Identify how Frank developed characters.
- ☑ Identify an irregular verb.
- ☑ Tell how revisions improved his writing.

Go Digital!
Write online in Writer's Workspace

313

? Essential Question

What excites us about nature?

Go Digital!

Nature!

Nature can be very exciting! This whale jumps out of the ocean many times a day. Some people write poems about what they see in nature. There are lots of nature topics to write about.

► The Outdoors

► The Seasons

► Living Things

Talk About It

Talk with a partner about what excites you about nature. List your ideas on the web.

Nature Excites Us!

Vocabulary

Use the picture and sentence to learn each word.

pale   Sam enjoyed looking at the **pale** yellow flowers.

What is the opposite of pale?

drops   There are **drops** of water on the plant.

Where else have you seen drops of water?

excite   The dancers will **excite** the audience.

What can excite you when you go outside?

outdoors   We played soccer **outdoors**.

Name something you can do outdoors that you cannot do inside.

Poetry Words

alliteration

I like to read a poem with **alliteration** because I like to say the same beginning sound in words.

Say three words with the same beginning sound.

repetition

Poets who repeat words or phrases in a poem are using **repetition**.

Why might a poet want to use repetition in a poem?

free verse

In **free verse**, the words do not need to rhyme.

Which would you rather write, a free verse or rhyming poem? Tell why.

simile

"Bill was as fast as a cricket" is an example of a **simile** because it uses the word *as* to compare two unlike things.

Name the two things that are being compared.

COLLABORATE

Your Turn

Pick three words and write a question about each for your partner to answer.

Go Digital! **Use the online visual glossary**

Snow Shape

? Essential Question

What excites us about nature?

Read how poets describe things in nature.

Snow is falling from the sky.
It gently lands on the ground.

It's bright, bright white, just like cold milk.
It looks so soft and smooth.

I hate to ruin it with my feet,
but I have got a plan.
I stand up tall and close my eyes,
and then straight back I fall.

I slide my arms up and down.
I move my legs in and out.

I stand up to see what I have made,
A four-foot shape in the snow
— Of me!

by Dana Williams

Nature Walk

When you take a walk in the fall,
leaves are like a blanket on the ground.
They crunch under your feet
with each step you take.

When you take a walk in the fall,
The air feels as cool as
drops of rain on your cheek.
It smells like clean cotton towels.

When you take a walk in the fall,
the outdoors will excite you.
It's a wonderful time!

by Sarah Miller

In the Sky

Outdoors on a clear day,
look up in the sky.
What do you see there?
Look! I see a giant polar bear.
Look! I see a pale flower growing.
Look! I see a buffalo and her baby.
Wait...it's changing.
Now I see a cowboy on his horse
Galloping, galloping across the sky.
I wonder where he'll ride?

by Juanita Marco

Make Connections

Talk about how nature excites the poet of each poem. **ESSENTIAL QUESTION**

Which poem do you like the most? How does it excite you about nature? **TEXT TO SELF**

Free Verse

Free verse poetry:
- tells a poet's thoughts or feelings.
- does not rhyme.
- can have similes.

Find Text Evidence

I can tell that "In the Sky" is a free verse poem. It tells the author's thoughts and feelings about the clouds. It also does not rhyme.

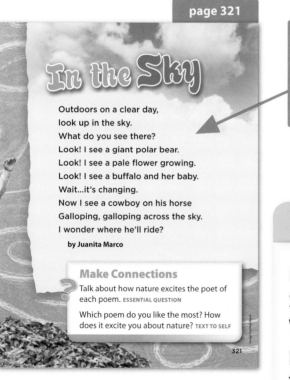

page 321

In the Sky

Outdoors on a clear day,
look up in the sky.
What do you see there?
Look! I see a giant polar bear.
Look! I see a pale flower growing.
Look! I see a buffalo and her baby.
Wait...it's changing.
Now I see a cowboy on his horse
Galloping, galloping across the sky.
I wonder where he'll ride?

by Juanita Marco

Make Connections

Talk about how nature excites the poet of each poem. ESSENTIAL QUESTION

Which poem do you like the most? How does it excite you about nature? TEXT TO SELF

321

This is a free verse poem. The lines do not end with words that rhyme.

COLLABORATE

Your Turn

Reread the poems "Snow Shape" and "Nature Walk." Explain why each poem is an example of a free-verse poem.

Theme

The theme is the main message or lesson. Identifying key details in a poem can help you figure out the theme.

Find Text Evidence

I'll reread "Nature Walk" and look for clues to figure out the theme of the poem.

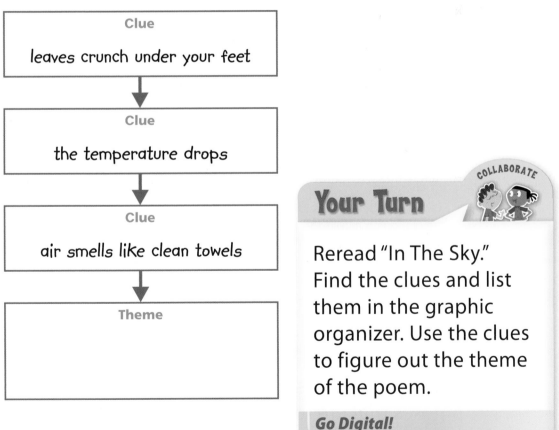

Clue

leaves crunch under your feet

↓

Clue

the temperature drops

↓

Clue

air smells like clean towels

↓

Theme

Your Turn COLLABORATE

Reread "In The Sky." Find the clues and list them in the graphic organizer. Use the clues to figure out the theme of the poem.

Go Digital!
Use the interactive graphic organizer

Repetition

Repetition is the use of repeated words and phrases. Poets use repetition to make a poem sound like a song or to stress the poem's meaning.

 Find Text Evidence

When I read "In the Sky" aloud, I can hear repetition. Reread the poem and listen for words that are repeated.

> page 321
>
> Outdoors on a clear day,
> look up in the sky.
> What do you see there?
> Look! I see a giant polar bear.
> Look! I see a pale flower growing.
> Look! I see a buffalo and her baby.
> Wait...it's changing.
> Now I see a cowboy on his horse
> Galloping, galloping across the sky.
> I wonder where he'll ride?

The poet repeats the word look. *It is followed by an exclamation mark. The repetition of this exclamation shows the excitement of finding shapes in the clouds.*

Your Turn

COLLABORATE

Reread "Nature Walk." Listen for words and phrases that are repeated. Talk about how the repetition adds meaning to the poem.

Design Pics/Alan Marsh

Similes

A simile compares two different things using the words *like* or *as*.

 Find Text Evidence

To find a simile, I need to look for a comparison of two unlike things. In "Nature Walk," the speaker compares leaves to a blanket on the ground.

page 320

Nature Walk

When you take a walk in the fall,
leaves are like a blanket on the ground.

Your Turn

COLLABORATE

Continue reading "Nature Walk." What other similes does the poet use? What two things does the poet compare in each simile?

(leaf) Ina Peters/Photodisc/Getty Images

Readers to . . .

Writers use sensory words to help the reader know how something looks, sounds, smells, tastes, or feels. Reread "Nature Walk."

Word Choice

Identify the **sensory words** in the poem. What sense does each word appeal to?

When you take a walk in
   the fall,
leaves are like a blanket
   on the ground.
They crunch under your feet
   with each step you take.

When you take a walk
   in the fall,
the temperature begins
   to drop.
The air feels as cool as
   raindrops on your cheek.
It smells like clean
   cotton towels.

Writers

Steven wrote a free verse poem.
Read Steven's revisions.

Editing Marks

(sp) Check spelling.

∧ Add

⁔ Take out.

Grammar Handbook

Contractions
See page 491.

Student Model

Day to Night

I like to watch the sky

change from day to night.

The sun ~~goes down~~ behind
(sinks)

the tall trees.

The clouds ~~are colorful~~.
(turn pink and orange)

Crickets make ~~noise~~ loudly.
(chirp)

My eyes feel heavy.

I can't keep them open.

Goodnight, (nighit) sky. (sp)

Your Turn

☑ Identify sensory
   words Steven used.
☑ Identify the
   contraction.
☑ Tell how revisions
   improved his
   writing.

Go Digital!
Write online in Writer's Workspace

Unit 5

Let's Make a Difference

The Big Idea

How can people make a difference?

"The world is like a great big puzzle and our job in life is to figure out where our piece fits. Mine just happens to fit with clean water. "

— Ryan Hreljac
Ryan's Well Foundation

Essential Question

What do good citizens do?

Go Digital!

Playground Fundraiser

Ryan Smith/Somos Images/Corbis

Good Citizens

These girls are raising money to buy playground equipment for a park in their neighborhood. They are good citizens. Citizens have rights and responsibilities.

▶ A citizen shows responsibility by keeping his or her neighborhood clean.

▶ A citizen has rights, such as the right to go to school.

Talk About It

Talk with a partner about other ways you can be a good citizen. Then write your ideas on the web.

Vocabulary

Use the picture and sentence to learn each word.

champion

Maya won the game and became the new **champion**.

What is a synonym for champion?

determined

The boy **determined** which books to check out at the library.

Who determined what you wore to school today?

issues

The fireman talked about **issues** of fire safety with the children.

What are some issues in your classroom?

promises

Zack and Jon made **promises** to tell the truth and stay friends.

Why should you keep your promises?

responsibility

It is my **responsibility** to clean my room every week.

What is a responsibility you have at home?

rights

Going to school is one of your **rights** as a citizen.

What other rights do you have?

volunteered

I **volunteered** to help plant flowers in the garden.

Tell about a time you volunteered to help someone.

votes

I wonder who got the most **votes** in our class election.

When do people use votes to decide things?

COLLABORATE

Your Turn

Pick three words. Write three questions for your partner to answer.

Go Digital! *Use the online visual glossary*

A Difficult Decision

Daniel Griffo

Essential Question

What do good citizens do?

Read about a boy who chooses to be a good citizen.

My best friend Paul and I were excited to go to the park after school. The park had a new fort. The Parks Department let the kids choose what kind of equipment to build, and the fort got the most **votes**. After school, Mom and I met Paul and his dad at the park.

Paul and I raced to the top of the tower. "I win. I'm the **champion**," I shouted. "Look, Paul! Someone left the newest GameMaster here. It's mine now!"

Paul raised his eyebrows and looked thoughtful. "Wyatt, you cannot keep that GameMaster," he said. "You have a **responsibility** to return it. It is your duty!"

I asked, "Haven't you ever heard the saying, 'finders keepers, losers weepers'? I have **rights**. I found it, so I am claiming it."

"You can do whatever you want, Wyatt, but you know it's wrong to keep it," Paul said. Then he added, "Whenever there are **issues** like this at school, you're the one who helps solve the problems. Now you aren't taking your own advice."

Then Paul added, "I **volunteered** my thoughts. If you don't want to take the help I offered, there's nothing I can do."

Paul was right. I couldn't keep the game because it wasn't mine. The person who lost it would be upset. I cleared my throat and said in my best deep voice, "I've **determined** that you're right!"

"I'm delighted you decided to do the right thing," said Paul.

We told my mother what happened. She walked around the park with us so we could try to find the owner of the game. Soon we saw a boy and his Mom looking for something. He looked hopeless, and he burst into tears when we asked him if the game was his. "Yes," he wailed, "I lost my GameMaster a little while ago. I should have been more careful!"

Afterward, Mom and I walked home. I was glad I returned the toy to the boy. So, I made a **promise** to myself to always try to do the right thing. Now that is a vow I can keep!

Make Connections

How are Paul and Wyatt good citizens? ESSENTIAL QUESTION

What is something you do to be a good citizen? TEXT TO SELF

Summarize

To summarize a story, you tell only the most important events of the story in your own words. This helps you remember what you have read.

Find Text Evidence

After reading page 335 of "A Difficult Decision," I can summarize what happens at the beginning of the story.

> **page 335**
>
> win. I'm the **champion**," I shouted. "Look, Paul! Someone left the newest GameMaster here. It's mine now!"
>
> Paul raised his eyebrows and looked thoughtful. "Wyatt, you cannot keep that GameMaster," he said. "You have a **responsibility** to return it. It is your duty!"
>
> I asked, "Haven't you ever heard the saying, 'finders keepers, losers weepers'? I have **rights**. I found it, so I am claiming it."

I read that Wyatt finds a hand-held game at the park and he wants to keep it. His friend, Paul, wants Wyatt to find the owner.

Your Turn

Summarize the middle and end of the story. Remember to tell the important events in your own words.

Daniel Griffo

Point of View

A character telling the story has feelings about the events. This is the character's point of view. The words *I*, *my*, *me*, and *mine* tell who is speaking.

 Find Text Evidence

When I read the second paragraph on page 335 of "A Difficult Decision," I can tell Wyatt is talking. I will look for clues to his point of view.

Character	Clue	Point of View
Wyatt	"It's mine, now!"	Wyatt thinks he should keep a game he found.

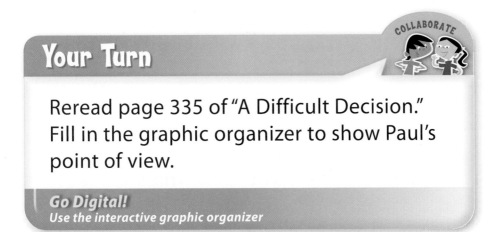

COLLABORATE

Your Turn

Reread page 335 of "A Difficult Decision." Fill in the graphic organizer to show Paul's point of view.

Go Digital!
Use the interactive graphic organizer

Realistic Fiction

"A Difficult Decision" is realistic fiction.
Realistic fiction:

- has characters that talk and act like real people.
- has a setting that could be a real place.
- can be told in the first person.

Find Text Evidence

I can tell that "A Difficult Decision" is realistic fiction. Wyatt and Paul could be real people. I also see that it is told by Wyatt, in the first person.

page 335

My best friend Paul and I were excited to go to the park after school. The park had a new fort. The Parks Department let the kids choose what kind of equipment to build, and the fort got the most **votes**. After school, Mom and I met Paul and his dad at the park.

Paul and I raced to the top of the tower. "I win. I'm the **champion**," I shouted. "Look, Paul! Someone left the newest GameMaster here. It's mine now!"

Paul raised his eyebrows and looked thoughtful. "Wyatt, you cannot keep that GameMaster," he said. "You have a **responsibility** to return it. It is your duty!"

I asked, "Haven't you ever heard the saying, 'finders keepers, losers weepers'? I have **rights**. I found it, so I am claiming it."

335

Story Structure

- The story uses first person **point of view**. The character uses *I*, *my*, and *me* to tell his thoughts and feelings.

Your Turn

COLLABORATE

Find two examples of how you know this story is realistic fiction.

Suffixes

To understand the meaning of a word you do not know, separate the word from a suffix, such as *-ful* or *-less*, to figure out the word's meaning.

 Find Text Evidence

I am not sure what thoughtful *means. The root word is* thought, *which has to do with thinking about something. I see the suffix* -ful, *which means "full of." I think the word* thoughtful *means "having a lot of thoughts."*

Paul raised his eyebrows and looked thoughtful.

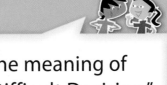 COLLABORATE

Your Turn

Use suffixes to figure out the meaning of the following words in "A Difficult Decision."
  careful, *page 337*
  hopeless, *page 337*

Daniel Griffo

Readers to . . .

Writers use descriptive details to tell about the characters, setting, and events. Reread the passage from "A Difficult Decision."

Ideas

What **descriptive details** does the writer include to help you understand Wyatt's actions?

Expert Model

Paul raised his eyebrows and looked thoughtful. "Wyatt, you cannot keep that GameMaster," he said. "You have a responsibility to return it. It is your duty!"

Writers

Maggie wrote a letter to her friend. Read Maggie's writing.

Editing Marks

≡ Make a capital letter.

⊙ Add a period.

∧ Add.

⌇ Take out.

Grammar Handbook

Pronouns See page 488.

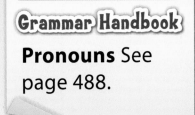

Student Model

Dear Talia,

    Yesterday was fun! My family and I went to the park. We worked with other people to pick up trash⊙∧≡ we wore gloves and used long poles to stick the trash. The park looked ~~good~~ _beautiful_∧ when we were finished!

Your friend,

Maggie

Your Turn

☑ Identify descriptive details Maggie used.

☑ Identify the pronouns.

☑ Tell how revisions improved her writing.

Go Digital!
Write online in Writer's Workspace

Let's Cooperate!

These kids are playing a game that takes cooperation. They have to interact and work together to make the parachute go up. To cooperate you need to:

► Listen and pay attention to those around you.

► Work together to do the task.

Talk About It

Talk with a partner about things you do that take cooperation. Then write your ideas on the web.

How We Cooperate

345

Vocabulary

Use the picture and sentence to learn each word.

amused

The kids told jokes and **amused** each other.

Describe something that has amused you.

cooperate

Runners must **cooperate** to win a relay race.

When have you had to cooperate at school?

describe

I would **describe** my cat as small and fluffy.

Describe what you are wearing today.

entertained

The funny clown **entertained** me.

Name something that has entertained you.

imagination

Ryan used his **imagination** to pretend he was in space.

Tell about something you see in your imagination.

interact

Mia likes to chat and **interact** with her friends at lunch.

Who do you like to interact with?

patient

The boy was **patient** and waited for his friend.

Tell about a time you have been patient.

peaceful

It was **peaceful** in the quiet library.

What is the opposite of peaceful?

Your Turn

COLLABORATE

Pick three words. Write three questions for your partner to answer.

Go Digital! **Use the online visual glossary**

SOCCER FRIENDS

? Essential Question

How do people get along?

Read about a girl who has a
problem on the soccer field.

Kelly couldn't wait until soccer season began. She could not be **patient** because she just loved racing to get the ball. She would use her **imagination** to picture the ball, and then she would fly toward it. Kelly practiced at home during the calm, **peaceful** mornings.

At the first team practice, Kelly greeted her friends. She liked to chat and **interact** with them. Then she saw a new girl. "That's Selena. She's a really fast runner," reported Kelly's friend Tara.

At first, Kelly held her tongue and said nothing. She was worried. She had always been the fastest runner on the team. Then she said, "I can beat her."

When practice started, Coach Troy had everyone line up for races. Kelly was nervous and had butterflies in her stomach.

"On your mark, get set, GO!" the coach shouted. Kelly ran as fast as she could but she noticed Selena getting ahead of her. Kelly tried her best but couldn't match Selena.

Later, Kelly watched as Selena **entertained** some girls by bouncing the ball on her head. The girls laughed, but Kelly was not **amused**.

That night, Mom could tell Kelly was upset. "Can you **describe** what's wrong?" she asked.

"A new girl named Selena beat me at the races. It stinks to get beaten!"said Kelly.

"I know that's disappointing for you," Mom said. "But it also sounds like good news for your team." Kelly thought about her Mom's words. She cared about the team, but she liked being the fastest.

At the next practice, the team played a game. Kelly and Selena were on the same team and Selena was goalie. She quickly blocked a goal.

Then Kelly got the ball and thumped it hard toward the net. She scored the winning goal!

After practice, Selena said to Kelly, "You were really great today."

"Thanks, so were you. I think our team can be great if we **cooperate** and work together," said Kelly.

"I think you're right about that," said Selena.

"I'd love to keep playing," Kelly said. "Want to come over to my house and practice?"

Make Connections

How does Kelly learn to get along with Selena on the soccer field? ESSENTIAL QUESTION

Compare Kelly's problem to a time you have had to work to get along with others. TEXT TO SELF

Summarize

To summarize a story, you tell only the most important events and details of the story in your own words. Use details from the story to summarize.

Find Text Evidence

After reading page 349 of "Soccer Friends," I can summarize what happens at the beginning of the story by retelling the key events and details.

page 349

Kelly couldn't wait until soccer season began. She could not be **patient** because she just loved racing to get the ball. She would use her **imagination** to picture the ball, and then she would fly toward it. Kelly practiced at home during the calm, **peaceful** mornings.

At the first team practice, Kelly greeted her friends. She liked to chat and **interact** with them. Then she saw a new girl. "That's Selena. She's a really fast runner," reported Kelly's friend Tara.

At first, Kelly held her tongue and said nothing. She was worried. She had always been the fastest runner on the team. Then she said, "I can beat her."

I read that Kelly is worried that the new girl on her soccer team will be a faster runner than she is.

Your Turn

COLLABORATE

Reread and summarize the middle and end of the story. Remember to tell the important events and details in your own words.

Richard Johnson

Point of View

Point of view is what the characters think about the events in a story. Look for clues about a character's point of view in the text.

 Find Text Evidence

On page 350, Kelly is upset that she lost the race to Selena. Kelly says, "It stinks to get beaten!" This is a clue to Kelly's point of view.

Character	Clue	Point of View
Kelly	*"It stinks to get beaten!"*	Winning is important.

COLLABORATE

 **Your Turn**

Reread page 351 of "Soccer Friends." Fill in the graphic organizer with Selena's and Kelly's points of view.

Go Digital!
Use the interactive graphic organizer

Fiction

The story "Soccer Friends" is fiction. **Fiction**:
- has made-up characters and events.
- has a problem and a solution.

🔍 Find Text Evidence

I can use what I read to tell that "Soccer Friends" is fiction. The characters and setting are made up. There is also a problem and a solution.

page 349

Kelly couldn't wait until soccer season began. She could not be **patient** because she just loved racing to get the ball. She would use her **imagination** to picture the ball, and then she would fly toward it. Kelly practiced at home during the calm, **peaceful** mornings.

At the first team practice, Kelly greeted her friends. She liked to chat and **interact** with them. Then she saw a new girl. "That's Selena. She's a really fast runner," reported Kelly's friend Tara.

At first, Kelly held her tongue and said nothing. She was worried. She had always been the fastest runner on the team. Then she said, "I can beat her."

When practice started, Coach Troy had everyone line up for races. Kelly was nervous and had butterflies in her stomach.

349

Story Structure

In the beginning of the story, I see there is a **problem**. Kelly is worried that the new girl on the soccer team might be faster than she is.

COLLABORATE

Your Turn

Continue rereading the story. Tell the solution to the problem.

Idioms

Idioms are words or phrases that have different meanings than the real meanings of the words. Look for clues in nearby words or sentences to find the meaning of an idiom.

 **Find Text Evidence**

I read that Kelly would 'fly toward the ball.' I know people cannot fly so this must be an idiom. Another sentence tells how Kelly enjoys racing to get the ball. I think this idiom means that Kelly moves quickly.

She would use her imagination to picture the ball, and then she would fly toward it.

Your Turn

COLLABORATE

Use context clues to figure out the meanings of these idioms in "Soccer Friends."

Kelly held her tongue, page 349
Butterflies in her stomach, page 349

Readers to...

Writers use short and long sentences to add interest to their writing. Reread the passage from "Soccer Friends."

Expert Model

Sentence Fluency

Identify **short and long sentences** the writer used to make the writing interesting.

At the next practice, the team played a game. Kelly and Selena were on the same team and Selena was goalie. She quickly blocked a goal.

Then Kelly got the ball and thumped it hard toward the net. She scored the winning goal!

Richard Johnson

356

Writers

Kent wrote a fiction story.
Read Kent's story.

Editing Marks

∧ Add.

⸝ Take out.

≡ Make a capital letter.

Grammar Handbook

Pronouns See page 488.

Student Model

Our Class Play

Our class put on a play for the school. ≡the play was "The Three Billy Goats Gruff." We all had parts in the play. I was the ~~the~~ littlest billy goat gruff. We all worked together to ∧^make^ the scenery and we practiced our lines a lot. It was a really great show!

Your Turn

COLLABORATE

- ☑ Identify long and short sentences Kent used.
- ☑ Identify the pronoun *I*.
- ☑ Tell how revisions improved his writing.

Go Digital!
Write online in Writer's Workspace

? Essential Question
What do heroes do?

Go Digital!

U.S. CO

Discover Heroes

What is a hero? A hero is someone who is looked up to by others because of his or her achievements and courage. A rescue worker is a hero to many people.

► Rescue workers risk their lives.

► Rescue workers save other people's lives.

Talk About It

Talk with a partner about who you think are heroes. Tell what they have done that makes them heroes. Write your ideas on the chart.

Hero	What Makes Them a Hero

Vocabulary

Use the picture and sentence to learn each word.

agree

Grandma and I **agree** to play a card game.

What is the opposite of agree?

challenging

This hard math problem is **challenging** to me.

Tell about something that is challenging to you.

discover

I dig in my backyard to **discover** buried treasure.

What are some things you would like to discover?

heroes

Fire fighters are **heroes** that help people.

What things make people become heroes?

interest

Adam has an **interest** in music.

Tell about an interest of yours.

perform

My class likes to **perform** songs at school.

Describe a time you saw someone perform in a movie or play.

study

I like to **study** the planets.

What things do you like to study?

succeed

I hope I **succeed** in winning the game.

What should you do if you do not succeed at something?

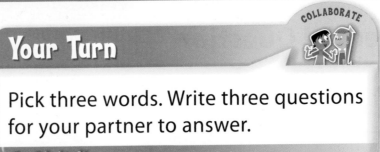

COLLABORATE

Your Turn

Pick three words. Write three questions for your partner to answer.

Go Digital! *Use the online visual glossary*

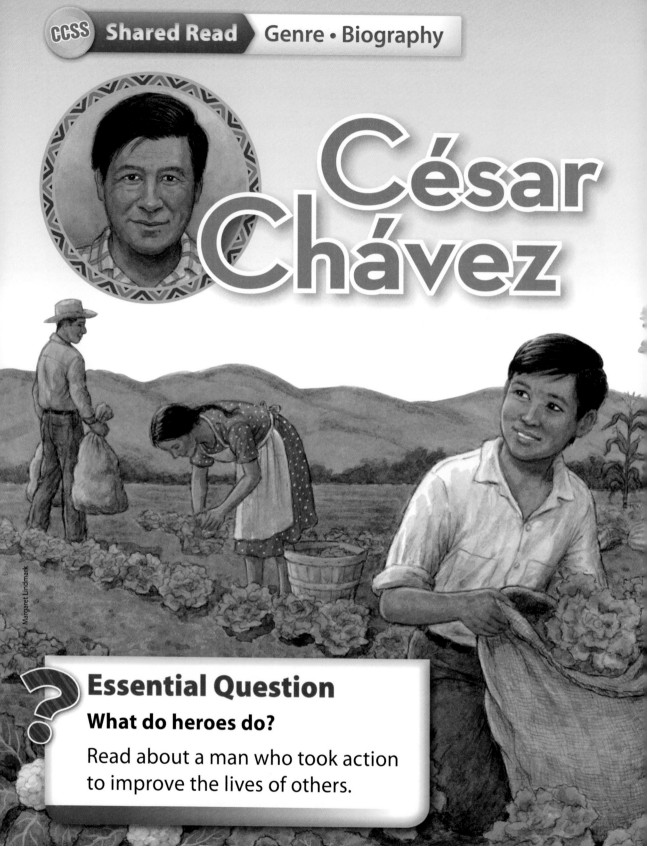

César Chávez

Margaret Lindmark

Essential Question

What do heroes do?

Read about a man who took action to improve the lives of others.

Who are your **heroes**? For many farm workers, César Chávez is a hero. He is the brave man who spent his life helping them.

Childhood

César Chávez was born in Arizona. His parents taught him about learning, hard work, and respect.

César worked on the family farm as a young boy. He helped care for the farm animals. His mother and grandmother taught César about caring. Many people came to their door asking for food, and his kind family always shared.

César had a strong **interest** in education. This desire to learn was sometimes hard on him. Spanish was his first language, but he needed to learn and **study** English. At school, he was punished for speaking Spanish.

His mother taught César to find peaceful ways to solve problems. These lessons helped him **succeed** later in life. He would win struggles without fighting.

Hard Times

When César was ten, it did not rain for a long time. This **drought** caused the plants on the farm to die. Without crops to sell, César's family couldn't afford to keep the farm.

Then César's family moved to California where there was no drought. His family traveled from farm to farm and worked the crops.

César and his family would quickly **discover** that migrant farm workers had difficult lives. Their **challenging** jobs forced them to work long hours for little money. The workers bent over all day tending the crops. The work they had to **perform** made their backs hurt and their fingers bleed. If workers complained, farm owners fired them.

Siede Preis/Getty Images

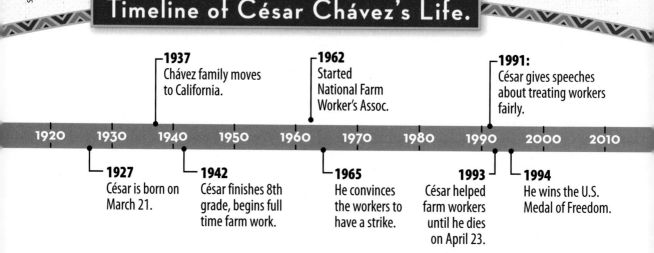

Timeline of César Chávez's Life.

1937
Chávez family moves to California.

1962
Started National Farm Worker's Assoc.

1991:
César gives speeches about treating workers fairly.

1920 1930 1940 1950 1960 1970 1980 1990 2000 2010

1927
César is born on March 21.

1942
César finishes 8th grade, begins full time farm work.

1965
He convinces the workers to have a strike.

1993
César helped farm workers until he dies on April 23.

1994
He wins the U.S. Medal of Freedom.

Changing Lives

César knew the migrant workers were not treated fairly so he decided to take action. He told the migrant workers he had a plan.

It was time for grapes to be harvested, or picked. César told the workers to stop working. This was a called a **strike**. The grapes began to rot. With no grapes to sell, the landowners lost money. Finally, the owners talked to César. They promised better pay. After that, the workers began picking the crops again.

César Chávez worked for the rest of his life to improve farm workers' lives. Would you **agree** that he is a hero?

Margaret Lindmark

Make Connections

How do César Chávez's actions make him a hero? ESSENTIAL QUESTION

How have you ever tried to help others? TEXT TO SELF

Summarize

Summarizing is using your own words to tell the most important events and details in a selection. This can help you remember new information in a selection.

Find Text Evidence

After reading page 365 of "César Chávez," I can summarize what happens in the section "Changing Lives."

---

page 365

Changing Lives

César knew the migrant workers were not treated fairly so he decided to take action. He told the migrant workers he had a plan.

It was time for grapes to be harvested, or picked. César told the workers to stop working. This was a called a **strike**. The grapes began to rot. With no grapes to sell, the landowners lost money. Finally, the owners talked to César. They promised better pay. After that, the workers began picking the crops again.

I read that César talked to other farm workers and they had a strike. When the owners promised better pay, the strike ended.

COLLABORATE

Your Turn

Summarize the section called "Childhood." Remember to tell the important events and details in your own words.

Sequence

The sequence tells the order of ideas in a selection. We can use the words *first*, *next*, *then* and *last* to tell the order of what happens.

 Find Text Evidence

As I read "César Chávez," I think about how the ideas and information are organized in the text. They tell the sequence of events in César's life.

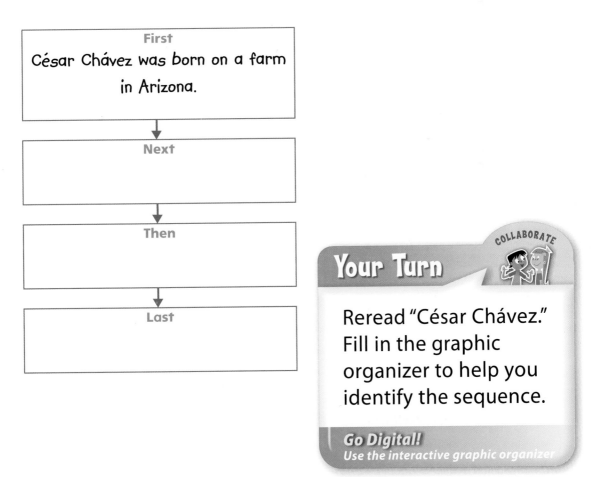

First

César Chávez was born on a farm in Arizona.

↓

Next

↓

Then

↓

Last

Your Turn COLLABORATE

Reread "César Chávez." Fill in the graphic organizer to help you identify the sequence.

Go Digital!
Use the interactive graphic organizer

367

Biography

"César Chávez" is a biography. A **biography**:
- is the true story of a real person's life.
- is written by another person.

🔍 Find Text Evidence

I can tell that "César Chávez" is a biography because it tells about the life of César Chávez. Another clue is that it has a timeline of his life.

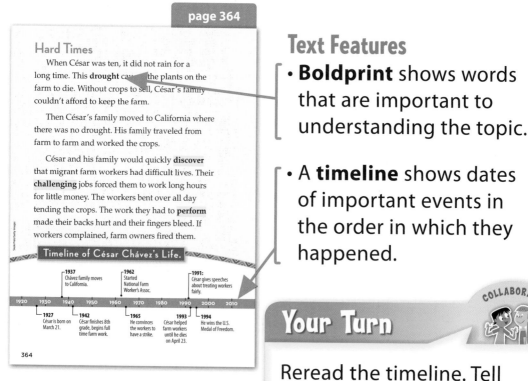

page 364

Hard Times

When César was ten, it did not rain for a long time. This **drought** caused the plants on the farm to die. Without crops to sell, César's family couldn't afford to keep the farm.

Then César's family moved to California where there was no drought. His family traveled from farm to farm and worked the crops.

César and his family would quickly **discover** that migrant farm workers had difficult lives. Their **challenging** jobs forced them to work long hours for little money. The workers bent over all day tending the crops. The work they had to **perform** made their backs hurt and their fingers bleed. If workers complained, farm owners fired them.

Timeline of César Chávez's Life.

1937 Chávez family moves to California.

1962 Started National Farm Worker's Assoc.

1991: César gives speeches about treating workers fairly.

1920 | 1930 | 1940 | 1950 | 1960 | 1970 | 1980 | 1990 | 2000 | 2010

1927 César is born on March 21.

1942 César finishes 8th grade, begins full time farm work.

1965 He convinces the workers to have a strike.

1993 César helped farm workers until he dies on April 23.

1994 He wins the U.S. Medal of Freedom.

364

Text Features

- **Boldprint** shows words that are important to understanding the topic.

- A **timeline** shows dates of important events in the order in which they happened.

COLLABORATE

Your Turn

Reread the timeline. Tell about events that happened in César Chávez's life.

Synonyms

Synonyms are words that have almost the same meaning. *Mad* and *angry* are synonyms. A synonym can be a clue to the meaning of another word.

Find Text Evidence

On page 363 of "César Chávez," I read the word caring. *In the last sentence of the same paragraph, I read the word* kind. Caring *and* kind *are synonyms.*

His mother and grandmother taught him about caring. Many people came to César's door asking for food, and his kind family always shared.

Your Turn

COLLABORATE

Find a synonym for these words in "César Chávez."

harvested, *page 365*
challenging, *page 364*

Readers to...

When writers tell facts about a person's life, they tell important events in order, or sequence. Reread the passage from "César Chávez."

Organization
How does the author use **sequence** to organize their writing?

Expert Model

It was time for grapes to be harvested, or picked. César told the workers to stop working. This was a called a strike. The grapes began to rot. With no grapes to sell, the landowners lost money. Finally, the owners talked to César. They promised better pay. After that, the workers began picking the crops again.

Writers

Editing Marks

/ Make a small letter.

∧ Add.

⌇ Take out.

¶ New paragraph.

Grammar Handbook

Possessive Pronouns
See page 489.

Jonathan wrote a biography. Read Jonathan's writing.

Student Model

Aunt Angela

My aunt, Angela, has always helped other people. First, when she was only ten, she had a lemonade stand. She did not keep the money. Instead, she gave it to her̶s̶ school. ¶ Today, ∧She volunteers at the hospital. She is always doing things for other people. I admire her.

Your Turn

COLLABORATE

- ☑ Identify a sequence word.
- ☑ Identify a possessive pronoun.
- ☑ Tell how revisions improved his writing.

Go Digital!
Write online in Writer's Workspace

Essential Question

How can we protect the Earth?

Go Digital!

Yi Lu/Corbis

Protecting the Earth

The Earth has many resources, such as water, air, and land. These children are protecting the Earth from pollution. Here are some other ways we can protect Earth's resources.

▶ Save water. Turn off the faucet while brushing your teeth.

▶ Keep the air supply clean. Have your parents turn off the car when they are waiting for someone.

Talk About It

Talk about ways you can help protect Earth's resources. Write your ideas on the chart.

Preserve the Earth.

Vocabulary

Use the picture and sentence to learn each word.

curious

I am **curious** to find out what is in the box.

Tell about something you are curious about.

distance

Lily waved from a **distance**, but her friend did not see her.

Tell about something that is at a distance from you right now.

Earth resources

Water and trees are important **Earth resources**.

What are some other Earth resources?

enormous

The bird looked tiny on top of the **enormous** rhinoceros.

What is another word for enormous?

gently The girls **gently** patted the puppy at the shelter.

Show how you would gently pat a kitten.

proudly Julia smiled **proudly** when she finished her painting.

Tell about a time you did something proudly.

rarely It **rarely** rains in the dry desert.

What word is the opposite of rarely?

supply The teacher has a **supply** of colored pencils for the class.

What else is there a supply of in the classroom?

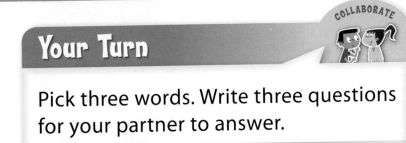

COLLABORATE

Your Turn

Pick three words. Write three questions for your partner to answer.

Go Digital! *Use the online visual glossary*

The Art Project

Art Contest

Kristen Sorra

❓ Essential Question

How can we protect the Earth?

Read to find out about saving Earth's resources.

"Look! The community center is having an art contest," said Grace. She was holding a flyer.

Mrs. Simon read the flyer aloud. Everyone agreed they would like to enter the art contest. Mrs. Simon said, "Our classroom **supply** of art materials is low because it's the end of the year. I'll check with Mrs. Rice to see what she has."

Mrs. Rice, the art teacher, didn't have any art materials. "I won't be getting a supply until next year," she said. The whole class was disappointed. "How can we enter the art contest without art materials?" asked Grace.

"Maybe we can raise some money. We could have a bake sale," suggested Hal.

"I don't think there's time," Mrs. Simon said.

"Let's use the paper in the recycling bin," Pablo said. Pablo did not often raise his hand. He **rarely** spoke up, so everyone was surprised when he offered an idea.

Hal said, "I'm **curious** about your idea. I want to learn why you would use old paper."

"So we can save **Earth's resources**," replied Pablo. "When we use recycled paper, we use natural materials and save trees."

"We can also use this old string and these wire hangers," added Grace.

Now the class had to decide what to do with the materials. Pablo had another idea. "We can fold the paper into cranes. Then we can attach the cranes to a frame to make a mobile."

Mrs. Simon taught the children how to fold the paper into cranes. Then everyone helped attach the cranes to the mobile.

Kristen Sorra

On the day of the art contest, the paper crane mobile hung in the **enormous** community center room. The huge space was crowded with art projects. From far off, the class spotted their project. The crane mobile swayed **gently** as people walked past. From a **distance**, the paper cranes appeared to be softly flying.

The judges checked each art project. They looked closely at the crane mobile.

The paper crane mobile won the prize for the most creative use of materials. As the class **proudly** accepted their prize, they could not stop grinning. Grace exclaimed, "We made our art project, and we saved the Earth at the same time!"

Make Connections

What do the children do at school to help protect the Earth? ESSENTIAL QUESTION

Tell about a way you can help protect Earth's resources at school. TEXT TO SELF

Make Predictions

Use what you already know and what you read in the story to predict what might happen next. Then you can confirm or revise your prediction.

Find Text Evidence

On page 377 of "The Art Project," I read that the class has no art materials. I predicted that they would ask kids to bring in the art materials. Then I read on to check my prediction.

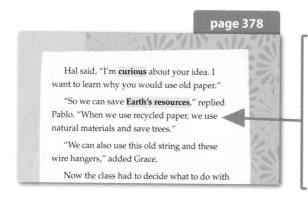

page 378

Hal said, "I'm **curious** about your idea. I want to learn why you would use old paper."

"So we can save **Earth's resources**," replied Pablo. "When we use recycled paper, we use natural materials and save trees."

"We can also use this old string and these wire hangers," added Grace.

Now the class had to decide what to do with

I read that the kids thought they could use recycled materials. This made me revise my prediction.

Your Turn

COLLABORATE

Reread page 378. What did you predict the children would do with the materials? Tell if you confirmed or revised your prediction.

Problem and Solution

The plot is often about the problem in the story. The solution is how the characters solve the problem by the end of the story.

 Find Text Evidence

On page 377 of "The Art Project," I learned the problem in the story. On page 378, I learned that Pablo suggested a step to solving the problem.

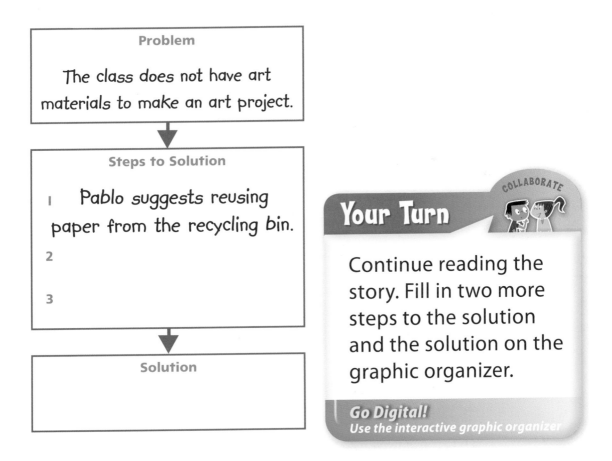

Problem

The class does not have art materials to make an art project.

↓

Steps to Solution

1 Pablo suggests reusing paper from the recycling bin.

2

3

↓

Solution

Your Turn COLLABORATE

Continue reading the story. Fill in two more steps to the solution and the solution on the graphic organizer.

Go Digital!
Use the interactive graphic organizer

Fiction

"The Art Project" is fiction. **Fiction**:

- tells a story about imaginary characters and events.
- includes a problem and solution.
- often includes dialogue.

Find Text Evidence

I know that "The Art Project" is fiction. It tells a story that includes a problem and a solution. It also has dialogue. The characters talk to each other.

page 377

> "Look! The community center is having an art contest," said Grace. She was holding a flyer.
>
> Mrs. Simon read the flyer aloud. Everyone agreed they would like to enter the art contest. Mrs. Simon said, "Our classroom **supply** of art materials is low because it's the end of the year. I'll check with Mrs. Rice to see what she has."
>
> Mrs. Rice, the art teacher, didn't have any art materials. "I won't be getting a supply until next year," she said. The whole class was disappointed. "How can we enter the art contest without art materials?" asked Grace.
>
> "Maybe we can raise some money. We could have a bake sale," suggested Hal.
>
> "I don't think there's time," Mrs. Simon said.
>
> "Let's use the paper in the recycling bin," Pablo said. Pablo did not often raise his hand. He **rarely** spoke up, so everyone was surprised when he offered an idea.

377

Story Structure

Dialogue is the words that the characters speak. The words are set inside quotation marks.

Your Turn

COLLABORATE

Find two more examples showing how you know this story is fiction.

Homophones

Homophones are words that sound the same, but have different spellings and different meanings.

Find Text Evidence

When I read the sentence on page 377, I'm not sure what the word "whole" means. I know that hole, spelled h-o-l-e, means "an empty space in something." Whole, spelled w-h-o-l-e, means "entire." I think the second meaning makes sense.

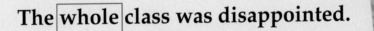

The whole class was disappointed.

COLLABORATE

Your Turn

Tell the meaning of the homophone as it is used in each sentence in "The Art Project."

see, *page 377*

won, *page 379*

Readers to...

Writers use linking words to show how ideas work together. These ideas can show a cause and an effect. Reread the passage from "The Art Project."

Expert Model

Word Choice
What **linking word** does the author use to show a cause and effect?

Mrs. Simon read the flyer aloud. Everyone agreed they would like to enter the art contest. Mrs. Simon said, "Our classroom supply of art materials is low because it's the end of the year. I'll check with Mrs. Rice to see what she has."

Kristen Sorra

Writers

Jade wrote a fiction piece.
Read Jade's writing.

Editing Marks

sp Check spelling.

𝒢 Take out.

∧ Add.

¶ New paragraph.

Grammar Handbook
Contractions
See page 491.

Student Model

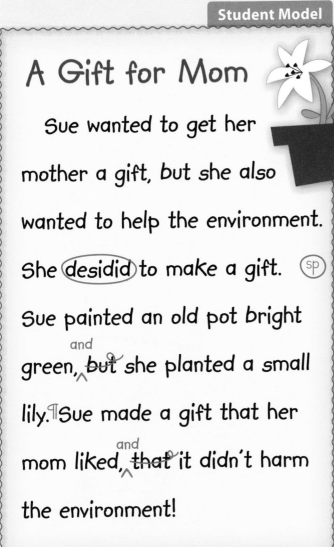

A Gift for Mom

Sue wanted to get her mother a gift, but she also wanted to help the environment. She desidid to make a gift. sp

Sue painted an old pot bright
and
green, ~~but~~ she planted a small
∧
lily. ¶Sue made a gift that her
and
mom liked, ~~that~~ it didn't harm
∧
the environment!

Your Turn
COLLABORATE

☑ Identify a linking word Jade used.
☑ Identify a contraction.
☑ Tell how revisions improved her writing.

Go Digital!
Write online in Writer's Workspace

385

Essential Question

Why are rules important?

Go Digital!

Rules

These children are going on a class trip. They are following the school's rules. They form two lines and listen to their teacher. Why do we have rules?

▶ Rules help keep us safe. By staying together, these children will not get lost.

Talk About It

COLLABORATE

Talk with a partner about rules you have at home. Then discuss why these rules are important. List your ideas on the chart.

Rule	Why It Is Important

Vocabulary

Use the picture and sentence to learn each word.

exclaimed

"What a surprise!" James **exclaimed**.

How do you think James felt when he exclaimed this?

finally

The mail is **finally** at Liam's house.

Why might Liam be happy that the mail has finally arrived?

form

Charlie and Dylan want to **form** a chess club.

What kind of club would you like to form?

history

Ben learns about the **history** of his family.

What do you know about the history of your family?

public

The school playground is Gina's favorite **public** place.

What public places do you visit in your town?

rules

We must follow the **rules** of our school.

Give an example of one of the rules of your school.

united

The children **united** to win the game.

Why is it important that they united in the game?

writers

The **writers** were busy finishing their stories.

Who are some of your favorite writers?

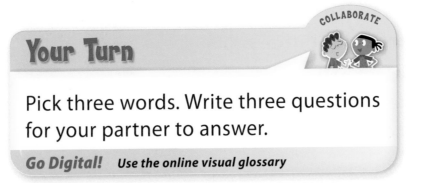

COLLABORATE

Your Turn

Pick three words. Write three questions for your partner to answer.

Go Digital! *Use the online visual glossary*

Visiting the Past

? Essential Question

Why are rules important?

Read about how America became an independent country and developed its own rules.

On the Fourth of July, skies across the United States light up. It's Independence Day! The holiday celebrates the Declaration of Independence.

The Changs visit Philadelphia.

In 1776, this statement was written to tell the King of England that the colonies were free from his rule. The colonies would be **united** to **form** a new country together.

Janet Chang, 8, recently visited Philadelphia with her family. Philadelphia was the first capital of the United States. The Changs went there to learn about their country's **history** or past.

Busy Building

First, they went to Independence Hall. "That's where the Declaration of Independence was signed," Janet **exclaimed**. She was excited to be there.

MIXA/Getty Images

Ten years after the Declaration of Independence, the Constitution was written in Independence Hall. The **writers** of the Constitution created new **rules** for the country. Rules are important. They help to keep order in a country and give people rights. One new rule was that people could state their opinion.

The signers of the Declaration of Independence.

Ringing for Freedom

The Changs later visited the Liberty Bell. It is said that the famous bell rang on July 8, 1776. That's when the first **public** reading of the Declaration of Independence took place. The bell also chimed to announce important events, such as when a President was elected.

Visit Philadelphia!

Famous Place	Why It Is Cool
The National Constitution Center	It explains the rules that were created for our nation. One area tells of the right to say what you want and the right to vote.
Independence Hall	This is where the Declaration of Independence and the Constitution were written. You can see the chair that George Washington sat in as he signed the Constitution.
Betsy Ross Home	It is said that Betsy Ross made the first American flag. You can tour her home to see how she lived and worked.

Memorable Moments

Finally, Janet and her family explored Franklin Court. This is where Benjamin Franklin lived and worked. Franklin was one of the writers of the Declaration of Independence. He also helped frame the Constitution.

To remember their visit, the Changs mailed a postcard from Franklin's post office. "I'll never forget this day!" Janet said.

Make Connections

What is one rule of our country? Why are rules important? ESSENTIAL QUESTION

How is this rule the same or different from your rules at school? TEXT TO SELF

Make Predictions

Use what you already know and what you read in the selection to help you predict what you will learn about. As you read, you can confirm or revise your predictions.

Find Text Evidence

After reading the title "Visiting the Past," I predicted the selection would be about a family visiting an important place from the past.

page 391

In 1776, this statement was written to tell the King of England that the colonies were free from his rule. The colonies would be **united** to **form** a new country together.

Janet Chang, 8, recently visited Philadelphia with her family. Philadelphia was the first capital of the United States. The Changs went there to learn about their country's **history** or past.

I read that the Chang family visited Philadelphia to learn about the past. I confirmed my prediction.

Your Turn

COLLABORATE

When you read the subheading "Ringing for Freedom", what did you predict would happen? Tell if you confirmed your prediction.

Cause and Effect

A cause is an event that makes something happen. An effect is what happens because of that event.

 Find Text Evidence

On page 391, I learn that Janet Chang and her family go to Philadelphia. That is a cause. I will read to find out the effects of their trip.

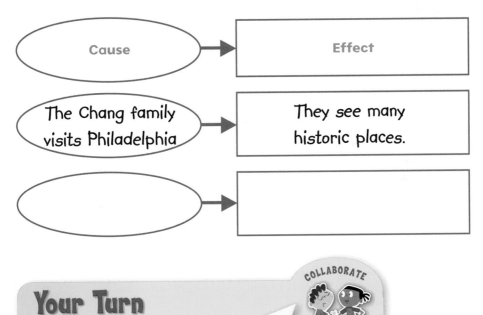

Cause	→	Effect
The Chang family visits Philadelphia	→	They see many historic places.
	→	

Your Turn

COLLABORATE

Reread page 392. Fill in the graphic organizer with a cause and effect.

Go Digital!
Use the interactive graphic organizer

Expository Text

"Visiting the Past" is an expository text.

Expository text:
- gives facts and information about a topic.
- can have photos, captions, and charts.

Find Text Evidence

I know "Visiting the Past" is an informational text because it gives facts about real places in the United States. It also has a chart that tells about these places.

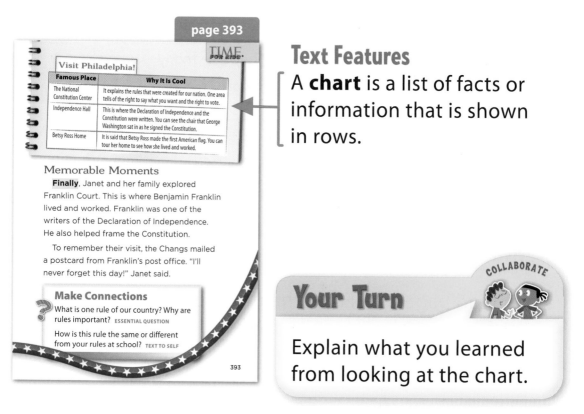

page 393

TIME FOR KIDS

Visit Philadelphia!

Famous Place	Why It Is Cool
The National Constitution Center	It explains the rules that were created for our nation. One area tells of the right to say what you want and the right to vote.
Independence Hall	This is where the Declaration of Independence and the Constitution were written. You can see the chair that George Washington sat in as he signed the Constitution.
Betsy Ross Home	It is said that Betsy Ross made the first American flag. You can tour her home to see how she lived and worked.

Memorable Moments

Finally, Janet and her family explored Franklin Court. This is where Benjamin Franklin lived and worked. Franklin was one of the writers of the Declaration of Independence. He also helped frame the Constitution.

To remember their visit, the Changs mailed a postcard from Franklin's post office. "I'll never forget this day!" Janet said.

Make Connections

What is one rule of our country? Why are rules important? ESSENTIAL QUESTION

How is this rule the same or different from your rules at school? TEXT TO SELF

393

Text Features

A **chart** is a list of facts or information that is shown in rows.

COLLABORATE

Your Turn

Explain what you learned from looking at the chart.

Multiple-Meaning Words

As you read, you may find words that could mean more than one thing. Look at the other words in the sentence to help you figure out which meaning is correct.

Find Text Evidence

On page 391 of "Visiting the Past," I see the word form. I know a form can be "a piece of paper." It can also mean "to make something." When I read the sentence, the meaning "to make something" makes sense.

> The colonies would be united
> to form a new country together.

Your Turn

Find these words in "Visiting the Past." Write the correct meaning based on the sentence the word is in.

order, *page 392*
state, *page 392*

Readers to...

Writers use a formal voice when the reader is a person such as a teacher. An informal voice is used when the reader is a family member or friend. Reread the passage from "Visiting the Past."

Expert Model

Voice
Identify the **formal** or **informal** voice in this paragraph. Why did the writer choose this voice?

On the Fourth of July, skies across the United States light up. It's Independence Day! The holiday celebrates the Declaration of Independence.

In 1776, this statement was written to tell the King of England that the colonies were free from his rule. The colonies would be united to form a new country together.

Writers

Caleb wrote an expository text. Read Caleb's revision.

Editing Marks

∧ Add

⸍ Take out.

¶ New paragraph.

Grammar Handbook

Pronoun-Verb Agreement
See page 490.

Student Model

Rules at Home

¶ At my house, we follow rules.

We does our homework before

watching TV. We go ^to bed at

8:00 p.m. We makes

our beds in the morning.

Each person follows the

rules. Following rules makes

our house run smoothly.

Your Turn

COLLABORATE

- ✔ Identify the voice of Caleb's writing.
- ✔ Find ways that Caleb fixed pronoun-verb agreement.
- ✔ Tell how revisions improved his writing.

Go Digital!
Write online in Writer's Workspace

How on Earth?

The Big Idea

What keeps our world working?

Our World at Work

Sun and rain and people too,
    Help our world keep turning.
Doctors work to make us well,
    Teachers help with learning.

Animals and plants give food,
    Farmers start things growing.
Electric power lights our world,
    Highways get us going.

Round and round and round we go,
    Growing and improving.
Sun and rain and people, too,
    Help our world keep moving.

by Charles Ashton

Essential Question

What do myths help us understand?

Go Digital!

Plant Myths

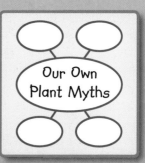

Do you know the myth about bluebells? It is thought that if you disturb them, something bad will happen. Some myths were created to help us understand how plants develop. Other myths help us understand the stages of a plant's life. Here are a few myths about plants.

▶ Finding a four-leaf clover is lucky.

▶ When a dandelion dies, you will get a wish when you blow away the seeds.

Talk About It   COLLABORATE

Create your own plant myths with a partner. Write your ideas on the web.

Our Own Plant Myths

Vocabulary

Use the picture and sentence to learn each word.

appeared Buds **appeared** on the tree in early spring.

What *else do you think* appeared in spring?

crops The farmer grows **crops** of corn and wheat.

What are *some other crops?*

develop The tadpole will **develop** into a frog.

What is another word for develop?

edge The ball rolled off the **edge** of the table.

Point to the edge of your desk.

golden

The **golden** sun shone in the blue sky.

Name some things that are golden.

rustled

The leaves **rustled** in the wind.

What else could make a rustling sound?

shining

The **shining** flashlight made it easier for us to read the book at night.

What else have you seen shining?

stages

Egg, caterpillar, and butterfly are **stages** in a butterfly's life.

What are the stages in a cat's life?

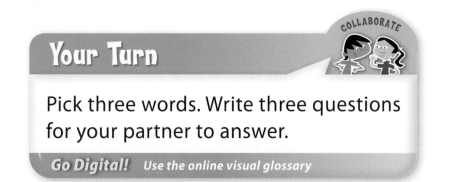

COLLABORATE

Your Turn

Pick three words. Write three questions for your partner to answer.

Go Digital! *Use the online visual glossary*

Why FirTree Keeps His Leaves

Xiao Xin

Essential Question

What do myths help us understand?

Read about a tree that learns why he does not develop like other trees.

Long ago, in ancient times, Mother Nature gave each tree a different purpose. However, she did not share her reasons with the trees.

Fir Tree had three friends—Maple, Oak, and Elm. During the first summer, they saw Bird and Squirrel play in Farmer's corn and tomato **crops**. The breeze blew and **rustled** their leaves. The **shining** sun warmed them.

Then the first fall arrived. Farmer harvested what he had grown. Maple, Oak, and Elm's leaves turned beautiful shades of orange, red, and yellow. The leaves shone as **golden** as the Sun. Fir Tree's leaves stayed green.

Fir Tree complained to Mother Nature, "I don't like my leaves. I want them to change colors like my friends' leaves."

"Be patient," Mother Nature replied. "You will learn your purpose."

So Fir Tree waited. The temperature dropped even more. Bird flew south, and Squirrel was nowhere around. Maple, Oak, and Elm lost their leaves, but Fir Tree's green leaves remained. Soon snow blanketed the ground.

Again, Fir Tree protested to Mother Nature. "Why am I different? Why don't I have **stages** and change like my friends? I seem to be stuck in one period of life!"

"Be patient," Mother Nature replied. "Soon you will **develop** an understanding of your purpose."

Just then, Squirrel **appeared** on the **edge** of the forest. She was cold. When she went inside the forest, she saw Maple. She asked if she could build a warm nest in his branches.

Xiao Xin

Maple said he didn't have any leaves. She asked Oak and then Elm. Both said the same thing as Maple. She was still bitterly cold.

Squirrel approached Fir Tree. "Excuse me," she said. "May I build a nest in your branches?"

"Yes, that would be nice," said Fir Tree. Squirrel ran up Fir Tree's branches, and she made her nest. Soon, she was warm, comfortable, and asleep.

Fir Tree finally understood that his green leaves provided a warm shelter for animals in the winter. From that moment on, Fir Tree was happy to be different. Still today, he remains proud of his evergreen leaves.

Make Connections

How did Fir Tree develop differently from his friends? **ESSENTIAL QUESTION**

When have you wanted to be like your friends? **TEXT TO SELF**

Reread

As you read, you may not understand a word, phrase, or explanation in a story. Stop and reread these parts to be sure you understand.

Find Text Evidence

I didn't understand why Fir Tree doesn't like his green leaves. I will reread page 407 of "Why Fir Tree Keeps His Leaves" to find out why.

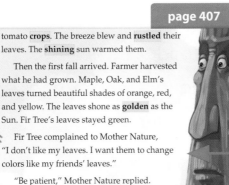

page 407

tomato **crops**. The breeze blew and **rustled** their leaves. The **shining** sun warmed them.

Then the first fall arrived. Farmer harvested what he had grown. Maple, Oak, and Elm's leaves turned beautiful shades of orange, red, and yellow. The leaves shone as **golden** as the Sun. Fir Tree's leaves stayed green.

Fir Tree complained to Mother Nature, "I don't like my leaves. I want them to change colors like my friends' leaves."

"Be patient," Mother Nature replied. "You will learn your purpose."

407

I read that Fir Tree saw the other trees leaves changing colors and he wanted his leaves to change colors.

Your Turn

COLLABORATE

Why can't Squirrel build a nest in Maple's tree? Reread page 409 to answer the question.

Theme

The theme of a story is the main message the author wants to tell the reader. To find the theme, think about what the characters say and do.

Find Text Evidence

On page 407 of "Why Fir Tree Keeps His Leaves," I read that Fir Tree is different from his friends. This clue gives me an idea about the theme.

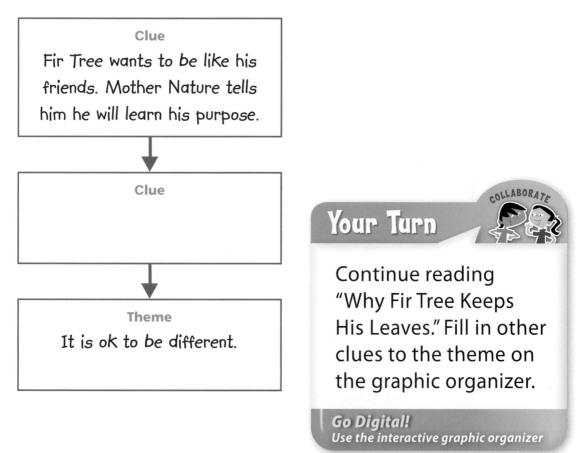

Clue

Fir Tree wants to be like his friends. Mother Nature tells him he will learn his purpose.

Clue

Theme

It is ok to be different.

Your Turn

COLLABORATE

Continue reading "Why Fir Tree Keeps His Leaves." Fill in other clues to the theme on the graphic organizer.

Go Digital!
Use the interactive graphic organizer

Myth

"Why Fir Tree Keeps His Leaves" is a myth.

A **myth**:

- is a made-up story.
- explains why things are the way they are.
- has an important lesson or message.

Find Text Evidence

"Why Fir Tree Keeps His Leaves" is a myth. I know the story is made-up. Trees and animals cannot speak. I also know it is a myth because the story explains why a fir tree is evergreen.

page 409

Maple said he didn't have any leaves. She asked Oak and then Elm. Both said the same thing as Maple. She was still bitterly cold.

Squirrel approached Fir Tree. "Excuse me," she said. "May I build a nest in your branches?"

"Yes, that would be nice," said Fir Tree. Squirrel ran up Fir Tree's branches, and she made her nest. Soon, she was warm, comfortable, and asleep.

Fir Tree finally understood that his green leaves provided a warm shelter for animals in the winter. From that moment on, Fir Tree was happy to be different. Still today, he remains proud of his evergreen leaves.

Make Connections

How did Fir Tree develop differently from his friends? ESSENTIAL QUESTION

When have you wanted to be like your friends? TEXT TO SELF

409

Genre Focus

A **myth** usually explains the lesson at the end. The end of this story explains why the fir tree never loses its leaves.

Your Turn

Talk with a partner about the lesson Fir Tree learned.

Context Clues

To understand the meaning of a word you do not know, look at the other words in the sentence for clues.

Find Text Evidence

I am not sure what harvested *means. I look at the other words in the sentence for clues. I read the words "what he had grown." I think* harvested *means something the farmer did after he grew his crops.* Harvested *must mean "picked" or "gathered."*

Farmer harvested what he had grown.

Your Turn

Use sentence clues to figure out the meaning of these words in "Why Fir Tree Keeps His Leaves":

complained, *page 407*
remained, *page 408*

Xiao Xin

Readers to...

Writers use a strong opening to get the reader's attention. They tell about the characters, setting and the problem the main character faces.

Expert Model

Organization
What do you learn in the **strong opening**? How does it set up the story?

Long ago, in ancient times, Mother Nature gave each tree a different purpose. However, she did not share her reasons with the trees.

Fir Tree had three friends—Maple, Oak, and Elm. During the first summer, they watched Bird and Squirrel play in Farmer's corn and tomato crops. The breeze blew and rustled their leaves. The shining sun warmed them.

Writers

Ethan wrote a myth about a plant. Read Ethan's writing.

Grammar Handbook

Adjectives

See page 492.

Student Model

Why the Rose Has Thorns

Long ago, Rose was a small

Her stem started to grow.

plant.∧ Rabbit came and bit her

stem. "Don't bite my stem!"

¶

Rose said. That night, while

sharp

Rose slept, she grew∧ thorns.

Rabbit came by and bit her

⊙

stem∧ "Ouch!" Rabbit said and

ran off. Rabbit never bothered

Rose again. She grew very tall.

Your Turn

☑ Describe Ethan's strong opening.

☑ Identify the adjectives.

☑ Tell how revisions improved his writing.

Go Digital!
Write online in Writer's Workspace

Essential Question

How do we use energy?

Go Digital!

Energy Sources

This boy is finding out information about the earth on his tablet. His tablet needs power to work. He charges the battery in his tablet with an electrical charger. Electricity comes from many sources.

▶ Electricity can come from solar power, wind power, and other sources.

Talk About It

How do you use energy at home? Talk with your partner and list your ideas on the chart.

Vocabulary

Use the picture and sentence to learn each word.

electricity The lights need **electricity** to work.

What other things need electricity to work?

energy It takes a lot of **energy** to power all the computers in our school.

What else at school uses energy?

flows The water **flows** from the tap into the sink.

What is another word for flows?

haul Dump trucks **haul** away big rocks.

What heavy things can you haul?

power

The windmills use wind to make **power** for homes.

What is another word for power?

silent

The classroom was **silent**.

When do you like it to be silent?

solar

This **solar** oven uses light from the sun to cook food.

Why might people want to use solar power?

underground

Prairie dogs live **underground**.

Tell about another animal that lives underground.

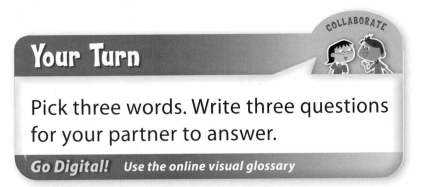

COLLABORATE

Your Turn

Pick three words. Write three questions for your partner to answer.

Go Digital! **Use the online visual glossary**

Pedal Power

People produce energy when they ride bikes.

Essential Question

How do we use energy?

Read about how people produce and use energy.

What Is Energy?

Energy is the ability to do work. **Solar** energy comes from the Sun. It's a **silent** source of energy, because it makes no sound. There is also energy that comes from wind and water.

Did you know that energy can come from people, too? When you pedal a bike, you produce energy. You use your legs to push the pedals. Your energy is transferred to the bike. This shift of **power** or energy makes the bike move.

Now imagine riding your bike to create enough power to run a computer. Some students at one school did just that! They hopped on bikes connected to generators and pedaled in place. Soon they were producing **electricity**. This energy is needed to run their laptop computers.

Bicycle-Powered Energy

Here's how bicycle-powered energy works. When a student pedals the bike, the rear wheel spins. The wheel spins the generator. The generator produces electricity.

As long as a student pedals the bicycle, electricity **flows**, or runs, through the generator. The electricity can be used right away. This energy can also be stored in a battery. It can be used later. Teachers can **haul**, or carry, laptop computers to the battery and plug them in for power.

Bicycle Generator

generator

battery

pedal

rear wheel

stand

Steve Schell

Using Bicycle-Powered Energy

People also exercise on bicycles and produce power in gyms. People create watts as they pedal. A watt is a unit for measuring power. Small devices, such as small televisions and fans, often use less than 100 watts per hour. These things can be run by bicycle-powered electricity.

It would be a mistake to use pedal power to run a refrigerator, though. This large appliance often uses more than 700 watts per hour. The electricity for these machines comes from power lines overhead or **underground**.

Pedal power is popping up in schools, gyms, and homes. What a fun way to provide electricity!

Bicycle power can be used to power these appliances.

Make Connections

How can people use the electricity they produce from riding bikes?
ESSENTIAL QUESTION

Tell about how you might use bike-powered electricity. TEXT TO SELF

(l) Dynamic Graphics Group/PunchStock; (b) Siede Preis/Photodisc/Getty Images

Reread

As you read, you may come across words, facts, or explanations that are new to you. Stop and reread these parts to be sure you understand them.

 Find Text Evidence

After reading page 422 of "Pedal Power," I wasn't sure how pedaling a bike makes electricity. I'll reread the page to find out.

page 422

Bicycle-Powered Energy

Here's how bicycle-powered energy works. When a student pedals the bike, the rear wheel spins. The wheel spins the generator. The generator produces electricity.

As long as a student pedals the bicycle, electricity **flows**, or runs, through the generator. The electricity can be used right away. This energy can also be stored in a battery. It can be used later. Teachers can **haul**, or carry, laptop computers to the battery and plug them in for power.

I read that pedaling a bike makes the wheel spin. The wheel spins the generator, which turns the energy into electricity. Now I understand how a bike makes electricity.

Your Turn

COLLABORATE

Reread "Using Bicycle-Powered Energy" on page 423. Explain how electricity made from pedaling a bike can be used.

Steve Schell

424

Author's Purpose

Authors write to answer, explain, or describe. As you read, look for clues to the author's purpose.

 Find Text Evidence

As I read "What Is Energy?" on page 421 of "Pedal Power," I'll look for clues that help me figure out the author's purpose. I'll write the clues in my chart.

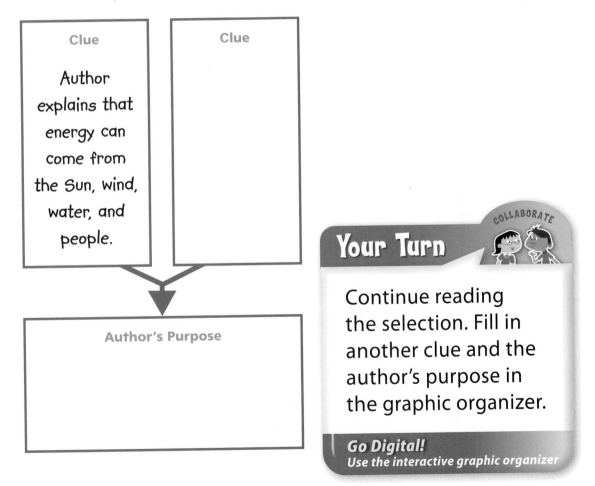

Clue	Clue
Author explains that energy can come from the Sun, wind, water, and people.	

Author's Purpose

Your Turn COLLABORATE

Continue reading the selection. Fill in another clue and the author's purpose in the graphic organizer.

Go Digital!
Use the interactive graphic organizer

Expository Text

"Pedal Power" is an expository text.

Expository text:
- gives facts and information about a topic.
- can include text features.

Find Text Evidence

I can tell that "Pedal Power" is an expository text. It gives information about people using bicycles to produce energy. It also has text features.

page 422

Bicycle-Powered Energy

Here's how bicycle-powered energy works. When a student pedals the bike, the rear wheel spins. The wheel spins the generator. The generator produces electricity.

As long as a student pedals the bicycle, electricity **flows**, or runs, through the generator. The electricity can be used right away. This energy can also be stored in a battery. It can be used later. Teachers can **haul**, or carry, laptop computers to the battery and plug them in for power.

Bicycle Generator

generator

battery

pedal

rear wheel

stand

422

Text Features

- **Subheadings** tell what a section of text is about.

- A **diagram** shows how something works. The **labels** give the names of parts or tell about actions.

Your Turn COLLABORATE

Look at the diagram and the labels. Tell what information you learned.

Paragraph Clues

You can use paragraph clues to figure out the meaning of a new word. Think about what you learned from the whole paragraph and use words you know to help you understand the new word.

Find Text Evidence

To figure out what the word transferred *means, I look at other sentences in the paragraph. Paragraph clues help me understand that* transferred *means "moved from one place to another."*

You use your legs to push the pedals. Your energy is transferred to the bike. This shift of power or energy makes the bike move.

Your Turn

COLLABORATE

Reread these paragraphs and tell what each word means, using paragraph clues.

stored, *page 422*
appliance, *page 423*

427

Readers to...

Writers often use science words when writing nonfiction to give the reader information about a topic. Reread the passage from "Pedal Power."

Word Choice

Identify two science words. How do these **content words** help you understand bicycle-powered energy?

Here's how bicycle-powered energy works. When a student pedals the bike, the rear wheel spins. The wheel spins the generator. The generator produces electricity.

As long as a student pedals the bicycle, electricity flows, or runs, through the generator. The electricity can be used right away. This energy can also be stored in a battery. It can be used later. Teachers can haul, or carry, laptop computers to the battery and plug them in for power.

Steve Schell

Writers

Paul wrote an expository text.
Read Paul's writing.

Editing Marks

(sp) Check spelling.

∧ Add

⌐ Take out.

≡ Make a capital letter.

Grammar Handbook
Articles
See page 492.

Student Model

The Sun

conserves

My family ~~saves~~ energy in
many ways. We turn off lights
when we are not using a room.
We enjoy reading or biking
instead of watching (telivision) (sp)
mom put in solar lights to light
the path to our house. These
things save electricity.

Your Turn

☑ Identify how Paul used content words.

☑ Identify an article Paul used.

☑ Tell how revisions improved his writing.

Go Digital!
Write online in Writer's Workspace

Essential Question

Why is teamwork important?

Go Digital!

Huntstock/Getty Images

Teamwork

These bikers are teaming up to explore nature. They are in a bike race in a park. Teaming up helps them in many ways.

▶ Teamwork helps them travel farther and faster than they could travel on their own.

▶ Teaming up keeps them safe. If someone gets hurt, there is someone there to help.

Talk About It

Think about jobs where people team up to explore. Then write your ideas on the web.

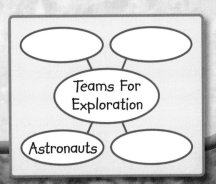

Use the picture and sentence to learn each word.

exploration We studied plants during our **exploration** of the forest.

Tell about what you might learn on an exploration of a beach.

important It is **important** to get a good night's sleep.

What are some important things to do in school?

machines **Machines** make it easier to cook in our kitchen.

Name some machines you have seen.

prepare Hitting balls helps Ben **prepare** for his baseball game.

How can you prepare for a big trip?

(t) Jupiterimages/Comstock Images/Getty Images; (tc) Ingram Publishing; (bc) Fuse/Getty Images; (b) George Doyle/Stockbyte/Getty Images

repair

The plumber will **repair** the broken sink.

Name some items that sometimes are in need of repair.

result

The tree fell over as a **result** of the storm.

What else might happen as a result of a storm?

scientific

Our **scientific** study helped us learn about rocks.

Tell what else you could learn from a scientific study.

teamwork

It takes **teamwork** to win a baseball game.

When have you needed to use teamwork? Why?

Your Turn

COLLABORATE

Pick three words. Write three questions for your partner to answer.

Go Digital! **Use the online visual glossary**

Dive Teams

Essential Question

Why is teamwork important?

Read about a team of divers who work together to explore a sunken ship.

Imagine exploring the underwater world of the ocean. Perhaps you want to see how sea animals live, or you may hope to search for sunken ships. That is just what Gloria did!

Gloria has always lived close to the sea in California. She swam and surfed at an early age. She became interested in the ocean. So Gloria became an expert diver. She decided to join a dive team to find sunken ships. What would her job be?

Each job on a dive team is **important**. One serious job is using **machines** the dive team needs. Another job is to **repair**, or fix, these devices when they don't work. Gloria is an experienced photographer, so she decides to photograph what the team discovers underwater.

Gloria and her team search for the sunken ship.

435

Teamwork is important for a dive team. Team members depend on one another. They divide up the tasks and each person helps to get the job done.

Gloria's team learns about a ship that sank over 100 years ago. No one has ever found it! They decide to make a **scientific** study of it. The team reads information and studies a map where they think the ship sank. They are excited about their **exploration**.

This map shows the route Gloria's team takes to the shipwreck.

The captain, another team member, takes them by boat to their map location. He stays on the boat where he can communicate with the divers.

Before the team dives, they **prepare** for their special jobs. To get ready, Gloria puts on her diving suit and gear and makes sure her camera is ready to take photographs.

Now the divers jump into the water. As they swim deeper, it gets darker. A team member turns on a flashlight. This helps the divers see where they are going.

Finally, one team member spots the ship! He uses an aquatic microphone to talk to the team. Gloria takes pictures as teammates measure the ship. Another teammate watches for sharks and other dangers.

After an hour of exploring, the person with the flashlight leads the way back to the boat. The team now has important **results** from their discovery to share. Gloria thinks, "I will always remember this dive!"

The team believes the ship Gloria heard about sank near other known shipwrecks off the coast of Florida.

Make Connections

Why is teamwork important for exploring shipwrecks? **ESSENTIAL QUESTION**

Would you enjoy being part of a team that explores shipwrecks? Explain your answer. **TEXT TO SELF**

Summarize

To summarize what you read, use your own words to tell the most important parts of a selection.

 Find Text Evidence

After reading page 435 of "Dive Teams," I can summarize what I read in my own words.

page 435

animals live, or you may hope to search for sunken ships. That is just what Gloria did!

Gloria has always lived in California, close to the sea where she swam and surfed at an early age. Soon she became interested in the ocean. So Gloria became an expert diver. She decided to join a dive team to find sunken ships. What would her job be?

Each job on a dive team is **important** . One serious job is using **machines** the dive team needs. Another job is to **repair**, or fix, these devices when they don't work. Gloria is an experienced photographer, so she decides to photograph what the team discovers underwater.

Gloria and her team search for the sunken ship.

I read that there are important jobs on dive teams and that Gloria decided to become an underwater photographer. From this, I understand that Gloria has an important job.

Your Turn

COLLABORATE

Reread the rest of the selection and summarize the ideas.

Main Idea and Key Details

The main idea is the most important point an author makes about a topic. Key details tell about and support the main idea.

 Find Text Evidence

As I read page 435 of "Dive Teams," I learned that there are many jobs on a dive team. This detail will help me find the main idea.

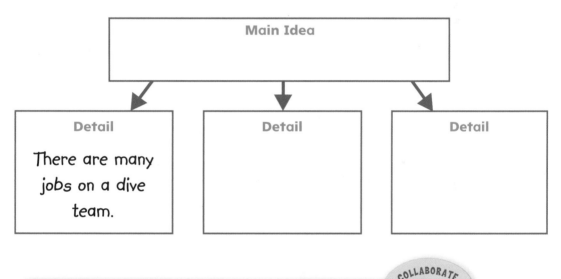

Main Idea

Detail	Detail	Detail
There are many jobs on a dive team.		

COLLABORATE

Your Turn

Continue rereading "Dive Teams." Add two key details and the main idea to the graphic organizer.

Go Digital!
Use the interactive graphic organizer

Expository Text

"Dive Teams" is an expository text.

Expository text:
- gives facts and information about a topic.
- may have photos, captions, and maps.

Find Text Evidence

I know "Dive Teams" is an expository text. It gives information about underwater teams. The text features help me learn how sunken ships are found and explored.

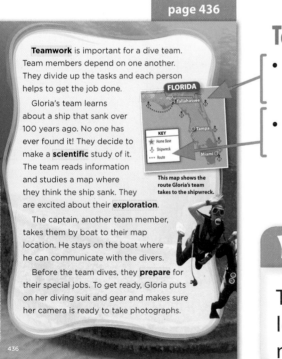

page 436

Teamwork is important for a dive team. Team members depend on one another. They divide up the tasks and each person helps to get the job done.

Gloria's team learns about a ship that sank over 100 years ago. No one has ever found it! They decide to make a **scientific** study of it. The team reads information and studies a map where they think the ship sank. They are excited about their **exploration**.

FLORIDA
Tallahassee
KEY
★ Home Base
⚓ Shipwreck
••• Route
Tampa
Miami

This map shows the route Gloria's team takes to the shipwreck.

The captain, another team member, takes them by boat to their map location. He stays on the boat where he can communicate with the divers.

Before the team dives, they **prepare** for their special jobs. To get ready, Gloria puts on her diving suit and gear and makes sure her camera is ready to take photographs.

436

Text Features

- A **map** is a flat picture of a part of the Earth.
- A **map key** tells you what symbols on a map mean.

COLLABORATE

Your Turn

Talk about what you learned from the map and map key in "Dive Teams."

Greek and Latin Roots

Word roots can help you understand what a new or unfamiliar word means. Many word roots come from the Greek and Latin languages.

 Find Text Evidence

I see the word divide. *I'm not sure what the word means. I know that* div *is a Latin root that means "separate." Divide* must mean *"separate something." That makes sense.*

They divide up the tasks and each person helps to get the job done.

Your Turn

COLLABORATE

Use the meaning of Greek and Latin roots to figure out the meaning of these words in "Dive Teams":

location, *page 436*

remember, *page 437*

Jeff Rotman/Photodisc/Getty Images

Readers to...

Writers choose details that support and explain the ideas in a selection. Reread the passage from "Dive Teams."

Ideas
What **supporting details** explain the idea that team members depend on each other?

Expert Model

Now the divers jump into the water. As they swim deeper, it gets darker. A team member turns on a flashlight. This helps the divers see where they are going.

Finally, one team member spots the ship! He uses an aquatic microphone to talk to the team. Gloria takes pictures as teammates measure the ship.

Writers

Lexi wrote an expository selection.
Read Lexi's writing.

Editing Marks

⊙ Add a period.

∧ Add.

ℐ Take out.

Grammar Handbook

**Adjectives
That Compare**
See page 493.

Student Model

Teamwork is Best

Explorers need to work as

a team⊙ When you explore, you∧

Before you begin exploring, you need a plan.
find out about someplace new.∧

learn
Do research to see∧ what you

can find. Decide what each

person's job will be. If you are

the strongest, you might carry

the heavy gear. Always listen

to your teammates!

Your Turn

COLLABORATE

- ☑ Identify supporting details Lexi used.
- ☑ Identify an adjective that compares.
- ☑ Tell how revisions improved her writing.

Go Digital!
Write online in Writer's Workspace

Weekly Concept Money Matters

Essential Question

How do we use money?

Go Digital!

MONEY

We use money in many ways. Money is used to purchase goods, or things, and services. This girl is using money to purchase a book, which is a good.

▶ We use money to buy other goods, such as food and clothing.

▶ We also use money to buy services, such as babysitting.

Talk About It

COLLABORATE

Talk with a partner about goods and services your family spends money on. List the items on the chart.

Goods	Services

(b, r) C Squared Studios/Photodisc/Getty Images

Vocabulary

Use the picture and sentence to learn each word.

invented

Thomas Edison **invented** the light bulb.

Tell about some other things people have invented.

money

Bills are **money** made of paper.

What coins do we use as money?

prices

Marsha looked at the **prices** of sneakers in the store.

Do you know the prices of any food items or toys?

purchase

Sam will **purchase** a snack at the fair.

What is another word for purchase?

record Our coach keeps a **record** of our positions on the field.

What is something you keep a record of?

system The teacher has a **system** for organizing our writing materials.

Tell about a system you have for doing something.

value A dollar has more **value** than a penny.

What coin has more value than a penny?

worth This television is **worth** a lot of money.

Name some things that are worth a small amount of money.

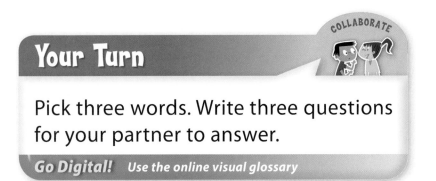

COLLABORATE

Your Turn

Pick three words. Write three questions for your partner to answer.

Go Digital! *Use the online visual glossary*

The Life of a Dollar Bill

Essential Question

How do we use money?

Read to learn about how a dollar bill circulates.

The Dollar Bill Is Printed

One day, a dollar bill is printed at the United States Bureau of Engraving and Printing. The bill is printed on a machine that was **invented**, or created, to save time. It prints many bills at a time.

The U.S. Bureau of Engraving and Printing prints millions of dollar bills each day.

Let's follow the dollar bill. It gets sent to a big bank and then a local bank. A family visits this neighborhood bank to get **money**. The dollar bill goes to a boy for his allowance.

The boy brings the dollar bill to the bookstore. He checks **prices** to see how much the books cost. Then he decides what he can **purchase**. He finds a book to buy, but is it **worth** the price? He's not sure. The boy reads the back of the book and thinks about the price. The boy decides the book is a good **value**, so he exchanges his money for the book.

The Dollar Bill Travels

Later, a girl buys a birthday card at the bookstore. She gets the dollar bill as change. She takes the dollar bill home and saves it in her piggy bank.

When the girl wants to see a movie, she takes money out of her piggy bank, including the dollar bill. She uses it to pay for the ticket. Then the dollar bill travels on.

Almost two years pass and now a man gets the dollar bill. It is worn out and torn. The man is not sure if it's usable. What happens to the ripped bill? The man takes it to his local bank and trades it in for a new dollar bill.

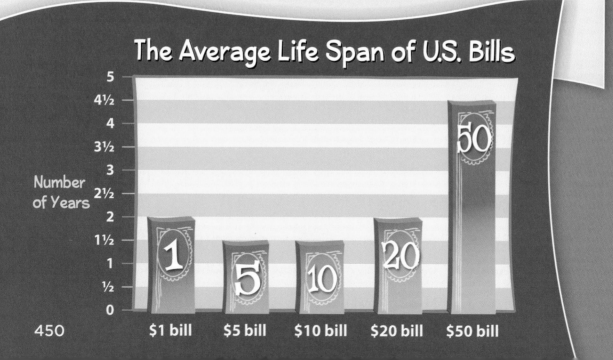

The Average Life Span of U.S. Bills

Number of Years

5
4½
4
3½
3
2½
2
1½
1
½
0

$1 bill $5 bill $10 bill $20 bill $50 bill

The Dollar Bill Is Replaced

The old dollar bill is returned to the big bank where workers decide that it can't be used again. They destroy the bill by shredding it. They cut it into tiny pieces.

Back at the U.S. Bureau of Engraving and Printing, a new dollar bill is printed to replace the old one. Workers use a **record** to keep track of how many bills are printed and destroyed. They make sure there are enough bills in the **system** so people can buy and sell things.

The next time you hold a one-dollar bill, think of where it has been and where it is going. Each dollar bill has a busy, useful life.

A machine shreds over 6 billion worn-out bills a year.

Make Connections

Why is a dollar bill important? **ESSENTIAL QUESTION**

What can you do with a one-dollar bill? **TEXT TO SELF**

Summarize

To summarize a selection, you tell only the most important details of the selection. This helps you remember what you have read.

Find Text Evidence

After I read page 449 of "The Life of a Dollar Bill," I will summarize what I read to make sure I understand it.

page 449

The U.S. Bureau of Engraving and Prin prints millions of d bills each day.

Let's follow the dollar bill. It gets sent to a big bank and then a local bank. A family visits this neighborhood bank to get **money**. The dollar bill goes to a boy for his allowance.

The boy brings the dollar bill to the bookstore. He checks **prices** to see how much the books cost. Then he decides what he can **purchase**. He finds a book to buy, but is it **worth** the price? He's not sure. The boy reads the back of the book and thinks about the price. The

> I read that a dollar bill is printed and first shipped to a big bank and then sent to a local bank. The dollar bill then goes to a boy and gets spent.

Your Turn

COLLABORATE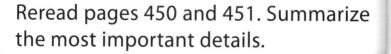

Reread pages 450 and 451. Summarize the most important details.

Problem and Solution

Some information in an informational text may be presented as a problem. The solution is how the problem is solved.

 Find Text Evidence

As I begin reading page 450 of "The Life of a Dollar Bill," I find a problem: Bills get worn out and torn. I keep reading to find the solution to this problem.

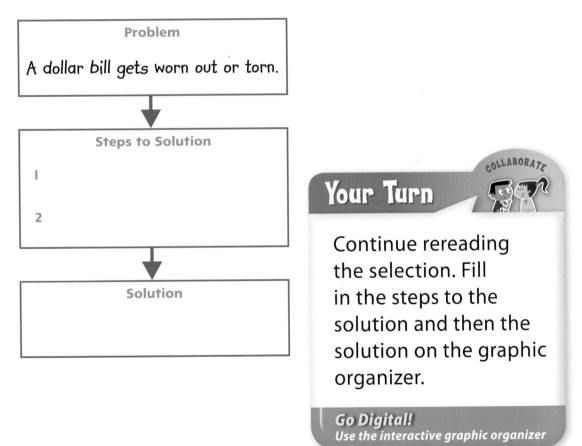

Problem
A dollar bill gets worn out or torn.

↓

Steps to Solution
1
2

↓

Solution

Your Turn COLLABORATE

Continue rereading the selection. Fill in the steps to the solution and then the solution on the graphic organizer.

Go Digital!
Use the interactive graphic organizer

Expository Text

"The Life of a Dollar Bill" is an expository text.

Expository text:
- gives facts and information about a topic.
- includes text features.

Find Text Evidence

I know that "The Life of a Dollar Bill" is an expository text. It gives information about money. The text features help me learn more about dollar bills.

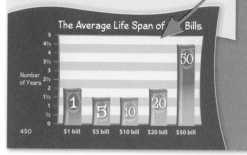

page 450

The Dollar Bill Travels

Later, a girl buys a birthday card the bookstore. She gets the dollar bill as change. She takes the dollar bill home and saves it in her piggy bank.

When the girl wants to see a movie, she takes money out of her piggy bank, including the dollar bill. She uses it to pay for the ticket. Then the dollar bill travels on.

Almost two years pass and now a man gets the dollar bill. It is worn out and torn. The man is not sure if it's usable. What happens to the ripped bill? The man takes it to his local bank and trades it in for a new dollar bill.

The Average Life Span of Bills

Text Structure

- **Subheadings** tell what a section of text is about.

- A **graph** helps you compare information using numbers.

COLLABORATE

Your Turn

Look at the graph. What information do you learn?

Paragraph Clues

Paragraph clues can help you figure out the meaning of a new word. Look at the sentences within the paragraph for clues to help you understand a new word.

🔍 Find Text Evidence

I'm not sure what the word shredding *means. In the first sentence the workers decide the dollar bill can no longer be used. The last sentence explains that shredding means cutting it into small pieces.*

> The old dollar bill is returned to the big bank where workers decide that it can't be used again. They destroy the bill by shredding it. They cut it into tiny pieces.

Your Turn

COLLABORATE

Reread these paragraphs and tell what each word means, using paragraph clues.

local, *page 449*

torn, *page 450*

Readers to...

Writers often include a strong conclusion in their writing. This ending can tell the main idea and gives the reader something to think about. Reread the passage from "The Life of a Dollar Bill."

Organization

Identify a **strong conclusion** in the text. How does this help organize the writing?

Expert Model

Workers use a record to keep track of how many bills are printed and destroyed. They make sure there are enough bills in the system so people can buy and sell things.

The next time you hold a one-dollar bill, think of where it has been and where it is going. Each dollar bill has a busy, useful life.

Kevin Zimmer

Writers

Sarah wrote an expository text. Read Sarah's writing.

Editing Marks

¶ New paragraph.

/ Make a small letter.

ℐ Take out.

∧ Add.

⊙ Insert a period.

Grammar Handbook

Adverbs

See page 494.

Student Model

Math and Money

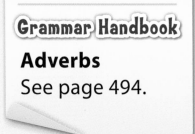

What do you do when you get money? You can save some of your money⊙ The rest goes into your pocket. You can buy a ℐnack. You pay with a dollar bill. You get twenty-five cents back.¶ Math and money ~~ever~~^always go together. Know your math and use your money wisely!

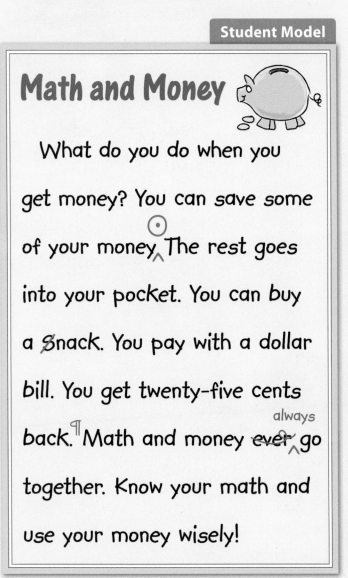

Your Turn

COLLABORATE

- ☑ Identify the strong conclusion Sarah wrote.
- ☑ Identify her correction of the adverb *ever*.
- ☑ Tell how revisions improved her writing.

Go Digital!
Write online in Writer's Workspace

Essential Question

Where can your imagination take you?

Go Digital!

Imagine!

Where have you gone in your imagination? What did you create? Your imagination lets you to do many things.

▶ You can do amazing things, like fly high in the sky.

▶ You can imagine becoming something, like a famous scientist.

Talk About It

COLLABORATE

Talk about something you like to imagine you could do. List your ideas on the chart.

We Imagine
We Can...

Vocabulary

Use the picture and sentence to learn each word.

create

The child will **create** a painting with paints.

What could you create with clay?

dazzling

The city lights looked **dazzling** at night.

What is something that you think is dazzling?

imagination

Bill used his **imagination** to be a pilot.

How have you used your imagination?

seconds

It took just a few **seconds** to run across the gym.

How many seconds does it take to do 20 jumping jacks?

Poetry Words

beats

The **beats** of a poem are the syllables that make rhythm in a line of poetry.

How many beats are in your name?

message

The poet used the poem to share her **message** about using your imagination.

What is the message in a poem you enjoy?

metaphor

"I'm a swan." is a **metaphor** because it compares two unlike things.

What is a metaphor you could use to describe yourself?

repeated lines

Sometimes poets use **repeated lines**. They include the same line at least twice in a poem.

Why might a poet want to use repeated lines?

COLLABORATE

Your Turn

Pick two words. Write a question about each word for your partner to answer.

Go Digital! **Use the online visual glossary**

A Box of Crayons

A box of crayons is the sun
on a dreary, rainy day.
You can draw a hot air balloon
and travel far far away.

You can draw a beach
and play in the silky sand.
You can draw a drum
and play in a marching band.

With crayons you can always create
something exciting, something great!

— by Isaiah Nowels

? Essential Question

Where can your imagination take you?

Read how poems share ideas and creativity.

Cat Zaza

What Story Is This?

None of us are us today,
We're putting on a play.

"Knock, knock, knock! Someone's there!"
That's the wolf, my friend Claire.

"Not by the hair of my chinny-chin chin!"
Julie, a little pig, says with a grin.

Joseph and Pat are pigs as well.
They run to Claire's house and ring the bell.
Do you remember this story's name?

If so, you've won this guessing game!

— by Trevor Reynolds

The Ticket

I have a special ticket
　　That takes me anywhere,
To oceans deep, the dazzling stars,
　　A mighty lion's lair.

I've been to a volcano,
　　Which is like a boiling pot,
I even rode a camel,
　　Through the desert, burning hot.

I've shivered in the North Pole,
　　At 43 below,
And built myself a cozy igloo,
　　Out of blocks of snow.

I've met a great inventor,
        And helped him to create,
A baseball playing robot,
        That slides into home plate.

My journeys take just seconds,
        I simply close my eyes,
And I'm a rocket sleek and silver,
        Speeding through the skies.

What's that? You'd like to join me?
        Here's all you have to do:
Use your imagination,
        And you'll soon go places, too!

— **by Constance Keremes**

Make Connections

Where does each poet go in his or her imagination? **ESSENTIAL QUESTION**

Which poem reminds you of somewhere you have been in your own imagination? **TEXT TO SELF**

Cat Zaza

Rhyming Poem

A **rhyming poem**:

- has words with the same sound at the end of some lines.
- has regular, repeating rhythm.
- tells a poet's thoughts or feelings.

🔍 Find Text Evidence

I can tell that "A Box of Crayons" is a rhyming poem, because it has pairs of lines that rhyme.

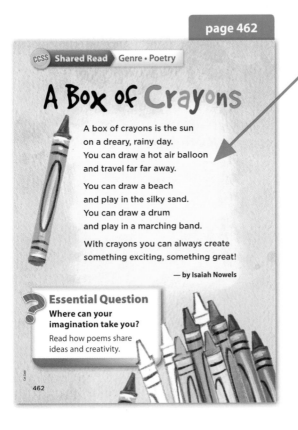

page 462

CCSS **Shared Read** ▸ Genre · Poetry

A Box of Crayons

A box of crayons is the sun
on a dreary, rainy day.
You can draw a hot air balloon
and travel far far away.

You can draw a beach
and play in the silky sand.
You can draw a drum
and play in a marching band.

With crayons you can always create
something exciting, something great!

— by Isaiah Nowels

Essential Question
Where can your imagination take you?
Read how poems share ideas and creativity.

462

A **verse** is a section of a poem or song. In this verse, lines two and four rhyme.

Your Turn COLLABORATE

Reread the poem "The Ticket." Decide which lines in this poem rhyme. Talk about the rhyming words.

Point of View

The way the speaker in a poem feels about something is his or her point of view.

 Find Text Evidence

When I read "A Box of Crayons" on page 462, I ask myself about the speaker's point of view.

Character	Clue	Point of View
speaker	A box of crayons is the sun/on a dreary, rainy day.	The speaker enjoys drawing with crayons on a rainy day.

 **Your Turn**
COLLABORATE

Reread page 465 of "The Ticket." Fill in the graphic organizer to help you identify the speaker's point of view.

Go Digital!
Use the interactive graphic organizer

Rhyme

Words that rhyme begin with different sounds but end with the same sound. Poets use rhyme and rhythm to give their poems a light feeling.

Find Text Evidence

As I read "What Story Is This?" on page 463 aloud, I can hear the rhyme. The rhyming words help the poem sound like a song.

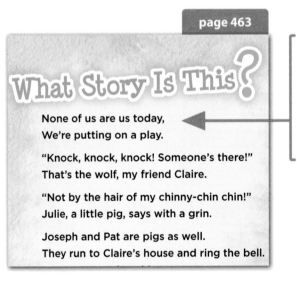

page 463

What Story Is This?

None of us are us today,
We're putting on a play.

"Knock, knock, knock! Someone's there!"
That's the wolf, my friend Claire.

"Not by the hair of my chinny-chin chin!"
Julie, a little pig, says with a grin.

Joseph and Pat are pigs as well.
They run to Claire's house and ring the bell.

The first and second lines rhyme. The rhyming words make the poem fun to read aloud.

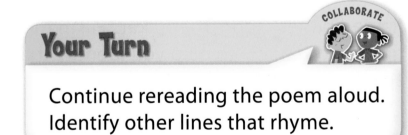

COLLABORATE

Your Turn

Continue rereading the poem aloud. Identify other lines that rhyme.

Cat Zaza

Metaphors

A metaphor compares two different things.
It does not use the words *like* or *as*.

Find Text Evidence

To find a metaphor, I need to look for two unlike things that are being compared. In "A Box of Crayons," the speaker compares a box of crayons to the sun. The metaphor is "A box of crayons is the sun on a dreary, rainy day."

page 462

A box of crayons is the sun
on a dreary, rainy day.
You can draw a hot air balloon
and travel far far away.

You can draw a beach
and play in the silky sand.
You can draw a drum
and play in a marching band.

With crayons you can always create
something exciting, something great!

COLLABORATE

Your Turn

Reread the poem "The Ticket" and identify a metaphor. Talk with a partner about what is being compared.

Cat Zaza

Readers to...

Writers use strong words, such as adjectives and adverbs, to make their poems interesting and clear. Reread "A Box of Crayons" below.

Word Choice

Identify the **strong words** the writer uses. How do they help you visualize what the speaker imagines?

A Box of Crayons

A box of crayons is the sun
on a dreary, rainy day.
You can draw a hot air balloon
and travel far far away.

You can draw a beach
and play in the silky sand.
You can draw a drum
and play in a marching band.

With crayons you can
         always create
something exciting,
something great!

Cat Zaza

Writers

Emilio wrote a poem.
Read Emilio's revisions.

Editing Marks

⊙ Add a period.

ⓢⓟ Check spelling.

∧ Add.

✐ Take out.

Grammar Handbook

Adjectives and Adverbs See pages 492, 494.

Student Model

My Box

strong, tall

I have a ∧box

that's not a box at all.

It's a rocket ship flying to

outer space.

ⓢⓟ
It's a castel protecting me

fierce
from the ~~mean~~ dragon.
          ∧

It's a boat bouncing over huge

ocean waves.

My sturdy, soaring box.

Your Turn

✔ Identify the strong words Emilio used.
✔ Identify the adjective Emilio replaced with a stronger word.
✔ Tell how revisions improved his writing.

Go Digital!
Write online in Writer's Workspace

Contents

Sentences

Sentences

A **sentence** tells a complete thought.

Tom feeds the cat.

Your Turn Write each group of words. Write "complete" next to the complete sentence.

1. The dog runs outside.
2. Digs in the yard.

Kinds of Sentences

Every sentence begins with a **capital letter** and ends with an **end mark**.

A **statement** tells something. It ends with a period.	*Tara can read music.*
A **question** asks something. It ends with a question mark.	*Do you like this song?*
A **command** tells someone to do something. It ends with a period.	*Sing along with me.*
An **exclamation** shows strong feeling. It ends with an exclamation mark.	*We sound great together!*

Your Turn Write each sentence. Then tell what kind of sentence it is.

1. Anna plays in a band.
2. Does she sing?
3. We love the new song!
4. Listen to the drums.

Subjects in Sentences

The **subject** in a sentence tells who or what does something.

Our teacher reads the story.

Your Turn **Write each sentence. Underline the subject.**

1. Ann listens to the news.
2. Mom looks outside.
3. Strong winds begin to blow.
4. Ann and Mom make plans.
5. The family prepares for the storm.

Predicates in Sentences

The **predicate** in a sentence tells what the subject does or is.

Our teacher reads the story.

Your Turn **Write each sentence. Underline each predicate.**

1. Rosa listens to the news.
2. She hears about the storm.
3. Her two brothers close the windows.
4. Everyone is excited.
5. The heavy rain falls at night.

Sentences

Combining Sentences: Subjects

When two sentences have the same predicate, you can use the word **and** to combine the subjects.

Trina <u>went to the movies</u>. Kim <u>went to the movies</u>.
Trina <u>and</u> Kim went to the movies.

Your Turn **Use *and* to combine each pair of sentences. Write the new sentence.**

1. Shawn sat down. Kent sat down.
2. Brianna wanted pizza. Kent wanted pizza.
3. The pizza smelled good. The pasta smelled good.
4. Kent asked for water. I asked for water.
5. Brianna thanked the waiter. Shawn thanked the waiter.

Nouns

A **noun** is a word that names a person, place, or thing.

My brother left his book at the library.

    ↑   ↑   ↑

  person   *thing*   *place*

Your Turn **Write each sentence. Draw a line under each noun.**

1. My family lives in a small town.
2. Our father works in the city.
3. The cousins share stories.

Common and Proper Nouns

Common nouns name general people, places, or things.

The <u>woman</u> drives her <u>car</u> down the <u>street</u>.

Proper nouns name specific people, places, or things.

<u>Jenny</u> walks <u>Whiskers</u> down <u>Park Street</u>.

Your Turn **Write each sentence. Underline each common noun. Circle each proper noun.**

1. My cousins are going to Mexico.
2. Their plane leaves from Chicago.
3. Lori will bring a camera.
4. My family will stay on Pine Street.

Nouns

Days, Months, and Holidays

Some proper nouns name **days of the week, months,** and **holidays.** They begin with capital letters.

Our homework is due on <u>Monday</u>. (day of the week)
My birthday is in <u>April</u>. (month of the year)
We will travel for <u>Thanksgiving</u>. (holiday)

Your Turn **Write each sentence correctly. Begin each proper noun with a capital letter.**

1. School is closed next monday.
2. It will be memorial day.
3. This was the warmest may ever.

Singular and Plural Nouns

A noun that names only one thing is **singular**.

A noun that names more than one thing is **plural**.

Add -*s* to form the plural of most nouns.

The large river split into two <u>rivers</u>.

Add -*es* to form the plural of nouns that end in *s, sh, ch,* or *x. This box is bigger than the other <u>boxes</u>.*

Your Turn **Write each sentence. Make the noun in ( ) name more than one.**

1. I have two (wish).
2. First, I need new (sock).
3. Next, I want three (book).

More Plural Nouns

If a word ends in a consonant plus *y*, change the *y* to *i* and add *-es* to form the plural.

> *My mother's <u>berry</u> pie has three kinds of <u>berries</u>.*

Some nouns change their spelling to name more than one. Others don't change at all.

Singular	Plural
man	men
woman	women
child	children
tooth	teeth
mouse	mice
foot	feet
fish	fish
sheep	sheep

Your Turn **Write each sentence. Make the noun in ( ) name more than one.**

1. The (child) went to a farm.
2. How many (sheep) did they see?
3. The barn was thirty (foot) high!
4. Four (pony) played in a field.
5. Workers picked (cherry) from the trees.

Nouns

Collective Nouns

A **collective noun** names a group that acts together as a singular thing.

The team runs out onto the field.

Your Turn **Write each sentence. Underline each collective noun.**

1. My family plays music.
2. I may start a band.
3. The group needs to practice.

Singular and Plural Possessive Nouns

A **possessive noun** is a noun that shows who or what owns something. Add an **apostrophe (')** and an -*s* to a singular noun to make it possessive.

The dog grabbed our father's hat.

Add just an apostrophe to most plural nouns to make them possessive. *The two brothers' bikes are both red.*

Add an apostrophe and an -*s* to form the possessive of plural nouns that do not end in -*s*.

The men went to get the women's coats.

Your Turn **Write each sentence. Use the possessive form of the noun in ( ) .**

1. I study at my (friend) house.
2. What are his (parents) names?
3. Listen to the (children) songs!

Action Verbs

An **action verb** is a word that shows action.

The runners <u>race</u> to the finish line.

Your Turn **Write each sentence. Draw a line under each action verb.**

1. We drive to the beach.
2. My father swims in the ocean.
3. My sisters build a sand castle.
4. My brother collects shells and rocks.
5. Mom dives into the water and splashes us.

Linking Verbs

A **linking verb** connects the subject to the rest of the sentence. It does not show action. Linking verbs include: *be, am, is, are, was, were, will be.*

Our teacher <u>is</u> a wonderful actor.

Your Turn **Write each sentence. Draw a line under each linking verb.**

1. The class play is a comedy.
2. The lines are hard to learn.
3. My best friends were clowns.
4. I am excited about my role.
5. The setting will be a circus.

Verbs

Present-Tense Verbs

Present-tense verbs tell what is happening now. Add -*s* or -*es* to tell what one person or thing is doing.

The man <u>looks</u> at the sky. He <u>watches</u> the dark clouds.

Your Turn Write each sentence in the present tense. Use the correct form of the verb in ( ).

1. The rain (start) to fall.
2. The horse (run) into the barn.
3. Water (rush) down the hill.

Past-Tense Verbs

Past-tense verbs tell about actions in the past. Most past-tense verbs end with -*ed*.

The players <u>kicked</u> the ball into the woods.

For verbs like *drop*, double the final consonant before adding -*ed*.

For verbs like *race*, drop the *e* before adding -*ed*.

The principal <u>tapped</u> the glass and <u>raised</u> the window.

Your Turn Write each sentence in the past tense. Use the correct form of the verb in ( ).

1. The coach (shout) at us.
2. We (stop) what we were doing.
3. The coach (dare) us to run another mile.

Future-Tense Verbs

Future-tense verbs tell about action that is going to happen. Use the verb *will* to write about the future.

Next year, my family <u>will visit</u> our relatives.

Your Turn **Write each sentence in the future tense. Use the correct form of each verb in ( ).**

1. We (drive) over five hundred miles.
2. My grandparents (be) happy to see us.
3. I (write) letters to all my friends.
4. We (call) each other when we can.
5. I (start) a journal and (take) many pictures.

Subject-Verb Agreement

A **subject** and **verb** must agree. Add *-s* or *-es* only if the subject tells about one person or thing in the present tense.

My <u>mother calls</u> us, and <u>we come</u> right away.

Your Turn **Write each sentence. Use the correct form of each verb in ( ).**

1. The hikers (climb) the mountain.
2. The guide (choose) a spot for the tent.
3. The group (rest) for a while.
4. The cook (start) a fire and (make) dinner.
5. Last year, they (camp) here as well.

Verbs

The Verb *Have*

Use **have** with most subjects in the present tense. For one person or thing, use **has**.

Use **had** for the past tense.

> *I have a red shirt. The girl has a blue shirt. We both had black shoes.*

Your Turn **Write each sentence. Use the correct form of the verb *have*.**

1. My mother (have) a question.
2. I (have) the answer.
3. Last fall, my sisters (have) a contest.

The Verb *Be*

For the present tense, use **is** if the subject is singular. Use **am** if the subject is *I*. Use **are** if the subject is plural or *you*.

For the past tense, use **was** if the subject is singular or *I*. Use **were** if the subject is plural or *you*.

> *Ann is the leader this year, but I was leader last year.*

Your Turn **Write each sentence. Use the correct form of the verb *be*.**

1. I (is) at the library.
2. You (is) at school.
3. Yesterday, Dad (is) at home.
4. Last week, we (is) all on vacation.

Contractions with *Not*

A **contraction** is a short form of two words. An **apostrophe** shows where one or more letters have been left out. Two irregular contractions are **can't** (can not) and **won't** (will not).

This isn't easy. You aren't ready. They don't want to go.

Your Turn **Write each sentence. Form a contraction using the words in ( ).**

1. My friend (did not) read the book.
2. The questions (are not) difficult.
3. Our teacher (does not) give us much time.
4. We (will not) finish before lunch.

Helping Verbs

A **helping verb** helps another verb show action. *Am, is* and *are* can help tell about action in the present. *Has* and *had* can help tell about action in the past.

Jess is telling a story. We had heard it before.

Your Turn **Write each sentence. Underline the helping verb.**

1. The boy is building a fort.
2. His father has helped him in the past.
3. We are watching them raise the roof.
4. Now I am bringing them lunch.

Verbs

Irregular Verbs

An **irregular verb** has a special spelling to show the past tense. Some also have a special spelling when used with the helping verb *have*.

Present	Past
come	came
do	did
eat	ate
give	gave
go	went
hide	hid
run	ran
say	said
see	saw
sing	sang
sit	sat
take	took
tell	told
write	wrote

Your Turn Write each sentence in the past tense. Use the correct form of the verb in ( ).

1. My friends (come) to my house yesterday.
2. Last weekend they (run) a race.
3. I (see) them training.
4. My friends (say) they would win.
5. They (go) fast and (do) well.

Combining Sentences: Verbs

When two sentences have the same subject, you can use the word **and** to combine the predicates.

Taylor swings the bat. *Taylor* hits the ball.

Taylor swings the bat <u>and</u> hits the ball.

Your Turn **Use *and* to combine each pair of sentences. Write the new sentence.**

1. My dad sings. My dad dances.
2. Paul claps. Paul stomps his feet.
3. Mother plays piano. Mother hums.
4. Jean is tired. Jean sits down.
5. We are having fun. We don't want to stop.

Pronouns

Pronouns: *I, You, He, She, It, We, They*

A **pronoun** takes the place of one or more nouns. The pronouns *I, you, he, she, it, we,* and *they* can be used as subjects in a sentence.

I like to ski. You and he like to surf.

Your Turn Write each sentence. Replace the underline word or words with a pronoun.

1. <u>My friend</u> lives near the beach.
2. <u>The house</u> is very small.
3. <u>Mom</u> has a sailboat.
4. <u>My friend and I</u> like to swim.
5. Are <u>his brother and sister</u> good swimmers, too?

Pronouns: *Me, You, Him, Her, It, Us, Them*

Some **pronouns** come after the verb in a sentence. The pronouns *me, you, him, her, it, us,* and *them* can be used in the predicate of a sentence.

Dad gave <u>him</u> the pen. He used <u>it</u> to write a poem.

Your Turn Write each sentence. Replace the underlined word or words with a pronoun.

1. We held <u>the fair</u> outside.
2. The rain soaked <u>the boys and girls</u>.
3. Who gave <u>my sister</u> an umbrella?
4. I saw <u>my father</u> inside his car.
5. An oak tree kept <u>my friend and me</u> dry.

Pronouns with *-self* and *-selves*

Some pronouns in the predicate tell about an action that a subject does for or to itself. The ending **-self** is used for singular pronouns. The ending **-selves** is used for plural pronouns.

The boy made <u>himself</u> a snack. We gave <u>ourselves</u> a pear.

Your Turn **Write each sentence. Replace the word or words in ( ) with a pronoun.**

1. My brother teaches (my brother) Spanish.
2. My mother asks (my mother) a question.
3. Could my parents teach (my parents) French?
4. The computer shuts (the computer) off.

Possessive Pronouns

A **possessive pronoun** takes the place of a possessive noun. It shows who or what owns something. *My, your, her, his, its, our,* and *their* are possessive pronouns.

I gave <u>my</u> homework to <u>our</u> teacher.

Your Turn **Write each sentence. Replace the underlined words with a possessive pronoun.**

1. <u>My sister's</u> room faces east.
2. She can see <u>the school's</u> playground.
3. <u>The building's</u> walls are made of brick.
4. <u>The teacher's</u> cars are parked nearby.
5. <u>My sister's and my</u> walk to school is short.

Pronouns

Pronoun-Verb Agreement

The verb of a sentence must agree with the pronoun that is the subject of the verb.

> *She laughs* while *we perform* our play.

Your Turn **Write each sentence. Use the correct present-tense form of the verb in ( ).**

1. She (draw) a map.
2. It (show) how to get to the lake.
3. We (hope) to get there by noon.
4. They (think) we may be lost.
5. Where (do) she think she is going?

Contractions

A **contraction** can be the short form of a pronoun combined with a verb. An **apostrophe** takes the place of the letters that are left out.

I'm sorry that you'll miss class today.

Your Turn **Write each sentence. Replace the underlined contraction with a pronoun and a verb.**

1. He's worried about the sick dog.
2. We're about to call the doctor.
3. Do you think she'll be able to help?
4. We hope it's not serious.
5. You'll soon feel better than ever!

Adjectives

Adjectives

An **adjective** is a word that describes a noun. Some adjectives tell what **kind** or how **many**.

Three dogs with <u>red</u> collars ran down the <u>dark</u> street.

Your Turn **Write each sentence. Circle each adjective and underline the noun being described.**

1. We'll need four apples for the pie.
2. Bake it for sixty minutes.
3. I prefer a thin crust.
4. Don't touch the hot plate!
5. Could I become a famous chef?

Articles

The words ***the, a,*** and ***an*** are special adjectives called **articles**. Use *a* before words that begin with consonant sounds. Use *an* before words that begin with vowel sounds.

<u>An</u> owl built <u>the</u> nest high in <u>a</u> tree.

Your Turn **Write each sentence. Circle the articles.**

1. A fox ran through our yard.
2. It woke up the dog.
3. I turned on a light outside.
4. A pair of eyes glowed in the dark.
5. I shut off the light in an instant.

This, That, These, and Those

This, that, these, and *those* are special adjectives that tell how many and how close. **This** and **that** refer to singular nouns. **These** and **those** refer to plural nouns.

I will read <u>these</u> books in my arms before I read <u>those</u> books on the shelf.

Your Turn **Write each sentence. Choose the correct adjective in ( ) to complete the sentence.**

1. My sister enjoys (this, these) movie.
2. I like (that, those) actors.
3. (This, These) special effects are great.
4. (That, Those) monster scared me.
5. I would watch (these, this) movie again.

Adjectives That Compare

Add **-er** to an adjective to compare two nouns. Add **-est** to compare more than two nouns.

Bill is <u>taller</u> than me, but Steve is my <u>tallest</u> brother.

Your Turn **Write each sentence. Add *-er* or *-est* to the adjective in ( ).**

1. My mom wants a (fast) car than our old one.
2. She looks at the (new) model of all the cars.
3. Does this car have a (high) price than that one?
4. This was the (hard) decision we've ever made!
5. Is one car is (safe) than another?

Adverbs and Prepositional Phrases

Adverbs

An **adverb** is a word that tells more about a verb. Adverbs tell *how, when,* or *where.* Many adverbs end in *-ly. We ran <u>quickly</u> to the front of the line.*

Your Turn **Write each sentence. Circle each adverb. Then underline the verb it tells about.**

1. I listened closely to the news.
2. The storm moved slowly out to sea.
3. We walked outside to check the sky.

Prepositional Phrases

A **preposition** comes before a noun or a pronoun. Together they make a **prepositional phrase**. Common prepositions include *in, at, of, from, with, to,* and *by.* A prepositional phrase can work as an adjective or an adverb that tells *how, when,* or *where.*

We ran quickly <u>to the front</u> <u>of the line</u>.

Your Turn **Write each sentence. Underline the prepositional phrase. Circle the preposition.**

1. I walked to the park.
2. Did you go with your friends?
3. We helped put trash in bags.
4. We did something good for our community.

Abbreviations

An **abbreviation** is a short form of a word. It usually ends with a period.

Main Street	*Main <u>St.</u>*
Lincoln Road	*Lincoln <u>Rd.</u>*
North Avenue	*North <u>Ave.</u>*
Apartment 6B	*<u>Apt.</u> 6B*
Mount Olympus	*<u>Mt.</u> Olympus*

Your Turn **Write each address using an abbreviation.**

1. 32 Front Street
2. 291 Jefferson Avenue
3. 7 Old Mill Road
4. Apartment 8H
5. 96 Mount Shasta Avenue

Titles

The abbreviation of a **title** before a name begins with a capital letter and ends with a period. Common titles before names are *Mr., Ms., Mrs.,* and *Dr.*

<u>Ms.</u> Choi invited <u>Dr.</u> Shaw and <u>Mr.</u> Howe to the show.

Your Turn **Write each name and abbreviation correctly.**

1. ms. Ellen Daly
2. Mr Mark Bryant
3. dr denise Putnam
4. mrs. june lee

495

Mechanics: Abbreviations

Days of the Week/Months of the Year

When you abbreviate the days of the week or the months of the year, begin with a capital letter and end with a period. Do not abbreviate *May, June,* or *July.*

Sun.   Mon.   Tues.   Wed.   Thurs.   Fri.   Sat.

Jan. Feb. Mar. Apr. Aug. Sept. Oct. Nov. Dec.

Your Turn **Write each sentence with the correct abbreviation.**

1. Our first meeting was on January 23, 2005.

2. The report is due on November 5.

3. Can you come to a party on April 17?

4. No one likes to meet on Saturday or Sunday.

5. We will meet again on Thursday, March 12.

States

When you write an address, you may use United States Postal Service abbreviations for the names of states. The abbreviations are two capital letters with no period at the end.

Alabama	AL	Kentucky	KY	Ohio	OH
Alaska	AK	Louisiana	LA	Oklahoma	OK
Arizona	AZ	Maine	ME	Oregon	OR
Arkansas	AR	Maryland	MD	Pennsylvania	PA
California	CA	Massachusetts	MA	Rhode Island	RI
Colorado	CO	Michigan	MI	South Carolina	SC
Connecticut	CT	Minnesota	MN	South Dakota	SD
Delaware	DE	Mississippi	MS	Tennessee	TN
District of		Missouri	MO	Texas	TX
Columbia	DC	Montana	MT	Utah	UT
Florida	FL	Nebraska	NE	Vermont	VT
Georgia	GA	Nevada	NV	Virginia	VA
Hawaii	HI	New Hampshire	NH	Washington	WA
Idaho	ID	New Jersey	NJ	West Virginia	WV
Illinois	IL	New Mexico	NM	Wisconsin	WI
Indiana	IN	New York	NY	Wyoming	WY
Iowa	IA	North Carolina	NC		
Kansas	KS	North Dakota	ND		

Your Turn **Write the U.S. Postal Service Abbreviation for each of the following.**

1. Chicago, Illinois

2. Dallas, Texas

3. Miami, Florida

4. Los Angeles, California

Mechanics: Capitalization

First Word in a Sentence

The first word in a sentence begins with a capital letter. A **quotation** is the exact words of a person speaking. The first word in a quotation begins with a capital letter.

<u>O</u>ur teacher said, "<u>R</u>emember to pack up your books."

Your Turn **Write each sentence. Use capital letters correctly.**

1. our coach talked to the team.
2. he said, "keep your eyes on the ball."
3. I asked, "can we practice our kicking?"

Letters

All of the words in a letter's greeting begin with a capital letter. Only the first word in the closing of a letter begins with a capital letter. Use a comma after the greeting and closing of a friendly letter.

Dear Sir,   *Yours truly,*

Your Turn **Write each part of a letter with the correct capitalization.**

1. dear mr. holland,
2. sincerely yours,
3. dear dr. andrews,
4. best wishes,

Names and Titles of People

The names of people begin with a capital letter. Titles begin with a capital letter. Always write the pronoun *I* as a capital letter.

Mrs. Walker and I built a bird feeder.

Your Turn **Write each sentence. Use capital letters correctly.**

1. Mr. taylor agreed to be our tour guide.
2. i think mrs. Shea is a better choice.
3. She knows dr. Peter miller.

Names of Places and Geographic Names

The names of streets, buildings, cities, and states begin with a capital letter. The names of rivers, mountains, countries, continents, and planets begin with a capital letter.

You can view Mars at Mount Evans Observatory in Colorado.

Your Turn **Write each sentence. Use capital letters correctly.**

1. We drive to washington to see the columbia river.
2. The river runs between portland and vancouver.
3. We may also visit mount st. helens.

499

Mechanics: Capitalization

More Proper Nouns and Adjectives

The names of schools, clubs, teams, and businesses begin with a capital letter. The names of products begin with a capital letter.

The Elmwood School Ramblers sell their Healthy Serving snacks at the bake sale.

The days of the week, months of the year, and holidays begin with a capital letter. The names of the seasons do not begin with a capital letter.

Labor Day is the first Monday in September.

Most abbreviations begin with a capital letter.

Mr. Ellis spoke with Dr. Garcia about his illness.

The first, last, and most important words in the title of a book, poem, song, story, play, movie, magazine, or newspaper begin with capital letters.

My father reads the <u>New York Times</u> while I watch <u>Alice in Wonderland</u>.

Your Turn **Write each sentence. Use capital letters correctly.**

1. This year february begins on a friday.

2. How will ms. davis celebrate valentine's day?

3. The mill river band is performing today.

4. The concert began with "america the beautiful."

End Marks

A **statement** is a sentence that tells a complete thought. It ends with a **period (.)**.

A **question** is a sentence that asks something. It ends with a **question mark (?)**.

A **command** is a sentence that tells someone to do something. It ends with a **period (.)**.

An **exclamation** is a sentence that shows strong feeling. It ends with an **exclamation mark (!)**.

Do you like black beans? They are my absolute favorite! I like them with rice.

Your Turn **Write each sentence. Add the correct end mark.**

1. We can make soup for lunch

2. Do we have enough vegetables

3. This soup will be the best ever

Periods

Use a period to show the end of an abbreviation. Use a period with initials that stand for a person's name.

On Oct. 23, Bill loaned me a book by C. S. Lewis.

Your Turn **Write each sentence. Use periods correctly.**

1. Mr Greco and his son joined us.

2. My mother read a book by j d salinger.

3. Oct and Nov are the best months to visit.

Mechanics: Punctuation

Commas

Use a **comma (,)** between the names of cities and states.

Austin, Texas   Albany, New York   Boston, Mass.

Use a **comma** between the day and the year in dates.

June 5, 1977   Sept. 18, 2010

Use a **comma** after the greeting and closing in a friendly letter.

Dear Grandma,   Best wishes,

Use **commas** to separate words in a series.

She took pictures of the alligators, otters, and parrots.

Use a **comma** after the words *yes* or *no* or the name of a person being spoken to.

Yes, I know Ben. Tracy, have you met him?

Use a **comma** after a sequence word.

First, we walk. Next, we take the bus.

Your Turn **Write each sentence. Add commas where needed.**

1. Dear Aunt Polly
2. I hope you like living in Portland Maine.
3. Were you born on July 4 1976?
4. Do you like parades picnics and fireworks?

Apostrophes

Use an **apostrophe (')** with a noun to show possession. Use an apostrophe in a contraction to show where a letter or letters are missing.

My brother's cat won't come in from the rain.

Your Turn **Write each sentence. Add apostrophes where needed.**

1. Our familys pets had a bad day.
2. The cats tail got stuck in the door.
3. Our dogs cant find their toys.
4. The door on the birds cage wont open.
5. Youll have to bring it to Mr. Swansons shop.

Quotation Marks

Use quotation marks at the beginning and at the end of the exact words a person says.

My uncle asked, "Where is your bike?"

"I left it at the shop," I replied.

Your Turn **Write each sentence. Add quotation marks where needed.**

1. My sister said, Your tire is flat.
2. I ran over some rocks, I replied.
3. She asked, What will you do now?
4. I need to get home right now! I exclaimed.
5. Can I borrow yours? I asked.

Mechanics: Punctuation

Italics or Underlining

Use italics or an underline for the title of a book, movie, magazine, or newspaper.

<u>James and the Giant Peach</u>   *Dolphin Tale*

Your Turn **Write each sentence. Use italics or underline the titles.**

1. I read the book My Side of the Mountain.
2. The magazine Film Fun said it was also a movie.
3. "Was it as good as The Incredible Journey?" you asked.
4. The Santa Monica Herald didn't think so.
5. Let's watch Finding Nemo again tonight.